Praying Like Crazy for Your Husband

Other books by Tamyra Horst

The Gift of Friendship

How to Hug a Heart

Praying Like Crazy for Your Kids

Ratty Bathrobes, Cranky Kids, and Other Romantic Moments

Time for All That's Important

A Woman of Worth

TAMYRA HORST

PRAYING LIKE CRAZY FOR YOUR HUSBAND

Pacific Press® Publishing Association
Nampa, Idaho
Oshawa, Ontario, Canada
www.pacificpress.com

Cover design by Steve Lanto

Cover resources from dreamstime.com

Inside design by Aaron Troia

Additional copies of this book are available by calling toll-free 1-800-765-6955 or visiting www.adventistbookcenter.com.

The author assumes full responsibility for the accuracy of all facts and quotations as cited in this book.

Library of Congress Cataloging-in-Publication Data:

Horst, Tamyra, 1961–

Praying like crazy for your husband / Tamyra Horst.

p. cm.

ISBN 13: 978-0-8163-2425-5 (pbk.)

ISBN 10: 0-8163-2425-5 (pbk.)

1. Wives—Religious life. 2. Christian women—Religious life. 3. Intercessory prayer—Christianity. 4. Husbands—Religious life. I. Title.

BV4528.15.H68 2010

248.3'2085'1—dc22

2010023357

10 11 12 13 14 • 5 4 3 2 1

Dedicated to Tim

I have prayed like crazy for you for the last thirty years

and will always pray for you.

Thank you for being patient and persevering with me

through the good and the tough.

I love you.

Contents

Marriages Follow Weddings

Every little girl dreams of the day. The white dress. The flowers. The walk down the aisle. The happily-ever-after.

As a teen she tests out her "married" name in the margins of her homework papers. Decides how many children she'll have—and decides if they'll be boys or girls or how many of each. (I wanted six. Three boys and three girls. What can I say? *The Brady Bunch* was one of the most popular shows on television at the time.)

She falls in love. Gets her heart broken. Falls in love again.

Then one day she meets "him." The man of her dreams. They date. Talk. Laugh. He proposes. She says Yes. Then comes months of planning. Pouring over *Brides* magazines. Talking with friends. Trying on dresses. Bridal showers. Agonizing over the flowers and menu. Wanting it all just right.

The day of her dreams arrives. She looks and feels like a princess. Her "prince" smiles as she walks down the aisle. The music. The vows. The candles. The moment that has taken "forever" to get here is over quickly, and they are walking breathlessly down the aisle, husband and wife.

And so begins a marriage.

Much planning and intentionality goes into the wedding. Often, less thought goes into preparing and living the marriage. Yet that's what it's all about. Marriage is a huge commitment. And a huge opportunity.

Commitment

For better or worse. In sickness and in health. For richer or poorer. Marriage is a commitment we make to one another. We promise that through good times and bad times, we will honor this commitment and make it work. Basically, our marriage vows promise, "I will love you no matter what."

But marriage is more than just a commitment to each other. In Christian marriages, we also make a commitment to God. We promise God that we will love our spouses no matter what. Good or bad. Easy or hard. We will work at this relationship and remain committed to it. We will make Him a part of the marriage and trust Him to guide us, give us strength, and show us how to love each other through it all.

It's not always easy. Wedding vows are almost a warning. There will be "worse" times, as well as good times. There will be days when money is tight and then moments when we can breathe easier financially. We will experience both good health as well as colds, the flu, and worse. God has not promised that marriage will be easy. But He has asked us to commit to loving each other through it all.

Opportunity

God knows that marriage is an opportunity. Especially in those moments when we stick it out through tough times. Whether the trials come from things outside of the relationship (job loss, financial problems, cancer), or when we're just not getting along and possibly feel wounded by the other, or we wonder where the love went.

Marriage is an opportunity to learn to love unconditionally. God loves us unconditionally and desires for us to love others with His love. We typically spend more time with our husbands and know them better than anyone else. This knowledge includes the irritating things. The things that bug and annoy us. We see their faults and bad habits. And we can learn to love them even when we don't like them.

Marriages Follow Weddings

Marriage is an opportunity to learn that love is more than a feeling. Feelings come and go. Love is an action. A verb. We *choose* to love. Sometimes it's easy to love. When he is nice, remembers to pick his clothes up off the floor, plays with the kids, or surprises us with flowers. Other times it's harder. He may be grouchy. Silent. Distant. He may work too much and not be around when we need him.

We can learn to *choose* to love in these moments too. And usually, when we love in action, the feelings follow. Learning to be loving when he's not grows us, causing us to let go of self and what we want, and to love unconditionally in the God who loves us. (This does not mean we need to remain in abusive relationships or that we should be doormats and not stick up for ourselves. If a relationship is abusive in any way—physically, emotionally, or mentally, seek help.)

One of the most loving actions we can do for our husbands is to pray like crazy for them.

We know them better than anyone else does. We know their gifts and talents, their struggles and sins. We know the things that challenge them and the areas in which the devil attacks them most frequently. We know their hopes and dreams—or whether they have none. We know their relationships, their work, their schedules. We also know their woundedness and the areas in which they most need healing. We know what they think is funny and who drives them crazy. We know how they like to waste their time off and what motivates them to work hard. No one else has the opportunity to know our husbands as intimately as we do.

We have committed before God to love this man, unconditionally, for always. Part of loving is praying. Prayer gives God permission to work. It deepens our love and commitment to our spouse. It allows us to partner with God for our spouse. To fight for him in spiritual warfare. To care about the things that he cares about, wrestles with, and dreams of.

Praying Like Crazy for Your Husband

We can pray for our husbands in ways no one else can because we know them like no one else does. I believe that praying for them is not just an opportunity—but a responsibility. Samuel told the children of Israel, "Far be it from me that I should sin against the LORD by failing to pray for you" (1 Samuel 12:23, NIV). Samuel believed that it would be a sin for him to not pray for these people for whom God had given him responsibility. I believe God desires wives to pray with this same commitment for our spouses. Because we know them more intimately and can pray more specifically, I believe our prayers can have an incredible impact on our husbands' lives.

Prayer changes things

In their book *Love and War,* John and Stasi Eldredge submit this challenge:

> Without you, your spouse will not become the man or the woman that God intends him or her to be and the Kingdom of God will not advance as it is meant to advance. Your spouse plays the most vital role in your life. You play the most critical role in your spouse's life. No one will have a greater impact on your spouse's soul than you. No one has greater access to your spouse's heart than you. This is an enormous honor. . . . You matter more than you thought. . . . We have been entrusted with the heart of another human being.[1]

A wife's prayers change things. They affect her husband. They impact his life. They give him courage, conviction, and strength. They help him to be the person God intended him to be. Husbands need our prayers. They need us to pray for them in ways they may not be praying for themselves, ways no one else will know how to. We can fight for them in prayer, helping them fight the battles they face each day.

Our prayers for our husbands also change us. They enable us to see the men who share our lives in different ways. As we pray specifically and like crazy, our love for them will grow and deepen.

Our love for our husbands will grow & deepen as we pray for them.

Sometimes when I've been mad at Tim, yet prayed for him, my own heart softened, the anger lessened, and God was able to help me understand, forgive, and better talk with him about whatever had happened. I remember being really angry at Tim one time. I don't remember the reason, but I was mad. Very mad. Instead of confronting him in anger, I decided to mow the grass. It needed mowing. It was physical. It was something Tim typically did, so I decided to do it for him to show love even though I wasn't feeling love. I figured maybe I could work out some of the anger.

While I mowed, I vented to God. Told Him whatever it was that Tim had done that made me so upset. I'm sure God got an earful. I'm wondering if He was smiling at me, chuckling a bit at the sight. I find it a bit amusing as I think about it now. I can see myself pushing the mower back and forth across the front yard just steaming mad. Yet as I prayed and mowed and vented, I calmed down. Because I was opening my heart to God, even in venting and complaining, God was able to speak, to soften my heart, to give me understanding, probably convicting me of some of my own faults, and helped me to forgive. In the end, Tim had a great looking front yard and a wife who was able to talk to him calmly and rationally.

Prayer changes husbands, but it also changes wives.

Prayer changes wives too.

Sometimes we just don't

As I've prayed through and worked on the ideas for

this book, I've been convicted that I don't always pray for my husband as I should. Yes, I sometimes pray like crazy, but I'm afraid many of my prayers are like the one when I was mowing. Hurt, angry, venting to God, complaining about whatever. Many times I'm just asking God to change Tim into the man I want him to be, instead of asking God to make him the man *He* created him to be. Selfish prayers.

I've prayed for Tim in a lot of ways, for a lot of different areas of his life and for a lot of things. Not everything has been selfish or complaining. I have battled in prayer for him in areas important to him and in ways he may never know. And I've often thanked God for this man He brought into my life about thirty years ago. There's a lot for me to be thankful for!

Yet as I've prayed about this book, I've realized again that wives have the opportunity to pray like no one else does. We can be "princess warriors" fighting for our husbands in prayer. There's a battle out there. Our husbands need to know that someone is on their side. Someone believes in them. Some days the battle may feel lonely and overwhelming. They need us, even if they don't realize it. Even if we don't realize it. God created us to be one. A team. Fighting for each other.

As wives, we have the unique opportunity and responsibility to pray like crazy and see God work in amazing ways.

Pray for:

- God to help you pray like crazy for your husband;
- God to deepen your commitment to praying for your husband;
- God to help you believe that your prayers make a difference;

- God to change you into the woman and wife He created you to be as you pray;
- God to help you pray specifically and intentionally for your husband;
- God to convict you of any ways your prayers may be selfish and not the way God desires you to pray for your husband.

for God to
block & resis
heart towa

I prayed all these prayers on 9-19-2017.

Journal

- How would you characterize your prayers for your husband? Have you been praying like crazy? Praying for God to change him into who you want him to be? Are your prayers selfish?
- How much intentionality have you put in your prayers for your husband?
- How have you seen God work in your husband's life as a result of prayer?
- How would you like God to change your prayer life or your prayers for your husband?

---

1. John and Stasi Eldredge, *Love and War: Finding the Marriage You've Dreamed Of* (Colorado Springs, Colo.: WaterBrook, 2009), 38, 39.

Love Well

In the last year or two, I've begun to pray that God will help me to "love well." I picked up the idea as I was reading through some of the New Testament in *The Message* paraphrase of the Bible. I read the phrase "love well" somewhere, and it stuck. I began to think about that phrase. Meditate on it. What does it mean to "love well"? Do I love Tim well?

It's been one of the priorities of my adult life to make sure that the guys in my life—my husband and two sons—know beyond a shadow of a doubt that I love them. I've told them daily—or more. I've tried to convey love by the things I've done for them, the little gifts and cards I've given them, the notes I leave for them. I've been intentional in my quest to make sure that they feel my love for them.

But have I loved well?

I recognized years ago that we all "hear" love in different ways. Tim and I even have been part of a team at church that preached on the five different love languages outlined in the books by Gary Chapman. We've talked as a family about the love languages, and each of us has identified how we best experience love. Armed with this insight, I've attempted to be intentional about "speaking" Tim's love language.

As a woman, I long to be loved well. I want Tim to be interested in me. Ask questions about my day and the projects I'm working on. I want him to *want* to spend time with me. I enjoy flowers and cards and cherish words of affirmation and encouragement. I'm a romantic. I do like long walks on a beach and candlelight dinners with soft music. I'm one of those mushy people who get teary-eyed when someone proposes in public. I even get teary-eyed during Hallmark card commercials!

Love and respect

God knew a woman's heart and her need to feel loved. He commanded husbands to love their wives. In Ephesians 5, He tells husbands that Christ gave the example of what such love looks like in the way He loved the church, giving Himself completely for the church to bring out the best of her—in essence, to bring out her beauty. Wow. That's how a woman wants to be loved! So completely that it makes her feel beautiful.

But God also knew a man's heart and what he needed to feel loved. In all the passages to husbands and wives, He never tells wives to love their husbands. Instead, He commands them to respect their husbands. Women long to be loved and cherished. Men want to be respected and honored. God knew. He created our hearts.

As author Shaunti Feldhahn surveyed men for her book *For Women Only*, she was surprised to learn how men responded when she asked about love and respect:

> Think about what these two negative experiences would be like: to feel alone and unloved in the world OR to feel inadequate and disrespected by everyone. If you were forced to choose one, which would you prefer? Would you rather feel alone and unloved or inadequate and disrespected?[1]

Those testing the survey questions on men reported that men didn't think that the question gave them choices. For men, to feel respected is to feel loved. To feel disrespected is to feel unloved. Men feel loved when they feel respected. But when forced to choose between love and respect, they will choose respect. Seventy-four percent of the men surveyed with the question said they'd rather be alone and unloved than inadequate and disrespected.

Our husbands will feel loved well when they feel we

For men, to feel respected is to feel loved. To feel disrespected is to feel unloved.

respect them. And not just when they earn it. They need our unconditional respect, just as we long for their unconditional love. Feldhahn writes, "Just as you want the man in your life to love you unconditionally, even when you're not particularly lovable, your man needs you to demonstrate your respect for him regardless of whether he's meeting your expectations at the moment."[2]

Showing respect

So my question, "Do I love Tim well?" becomes, "Do I respect Tim well?" Do I "speak" respect through my actions and words? Does he believe that I respect him for who he is apart from what he does? Are there ways he feels I don't respect him? These are all questions I take to God, asking Him not only to show me how to truly respect my husband but asking Him to reveal things I do or say that cause Tim to feel disrespected.

Knowing that he needs to feel my respect just as I need to feel his love nudges me to look for ways to speak respect to him. It will require more than just saying, "I respect you." It requires intentional action and thought. And an awareness of when he might feel that I lack respect for him.

I need God's help to be aware. Most of us do.

"I didn't realize that Jim was feeling disrespected," Sharon explains. "I was just teasing. The dishwasher broke, and he said he was going to take a look at it. I joked that if he looked at it, the repairman's bill was going to be higher. I didn't really mean anything bad by it. He's a great guy. I totally respect him. But the look on his face—I just knew I had blown it." When Sharon and Jim talked about it later, he explained that the teasing made him feel that she didn't really believe in his abilities. He would be the first to admit that his mechanical skills weren't great, but he wanted to look at it and make the phone call. He needed her to believe in him.

Love Well

I have a built-in reflex that whenever someone is complaining about another person, I tend to try to "help" the person complaining "see" or understand the other person. It's part of my longing to see people get along and like each other and not have conflict. Tim doesn't always see it as helpful. (And I'm sure it's not always helpful.) Instead, when he's talking about one of our sons and I start trying to help him see the situation from the son's viewpoint, Tim feels as if I'm defending our son instead of respecting or understanding his thoughts and feelings. He's had to say, "I don't feel respected when you do that."

I had no clue. I do respect my husband. He is an intelligent, hardworking man of integrity. I don't want him to feel that I disrespect him. And so I pray and ask God to convict me, to help me see things through Tim's eyes and know when I'm disrespecting him.

I've also told Tim that I never want him to feel disrespected and have asked him to tell me when he feels that way. But that requires prayer, too, because I'm not always open to his telling me things about myself. I want to argue and defend myself and say, "I'm not being disrespectful," which could cause him to not attempt to tell me next time. So I ask God to help me to really hear Tim and respond well, to allow God to use Tim to reveal how I do not love well.

Husbands will think we wives are being disrespectful when we're not trying to be. Teasing. Questioning their decisions. Nagging. When we complain about things not getting done around the house or about not having things that we want, they hear us saying they're a failure for not getting things done and not providing well enough for us.

I love taking care of my guys. I especially enjoy cooking for them. So I feel a little bad when I have to be away and they need to fend for themselves. For way too long, I'd tell them what they could fix or how to do it—out of my own sense that I wasn't taking care of them the way I should, not because I thought they couldn't figure it out on their own. One day Tim finally said, "I know how to fix dinner." In my need to "take care" of them, the message being conveyed was, "You don't know how to do this." I was trying to convey love, but he was hearing disrespect.

Because men and women are wired differently, we don't see or think from the same viewpoint. Ask God to help you be aware of how your husband might be hearing your words or actions. Are there ways you are really meaning one thing but he's hearing another?

Praying like crazy for me

So a book about praying like crazy for our husbands begins with a chapter on praying for ourselves and how well we love and respect our husbands. It's a challenge to truly love well and show respect. We think differently from our husbands. Experience things differently. We interpret things differently. Not just because we're men and women but also because of our past experiences, our own wounds and insecurities, our personalities, and how we think. Sometimes it's amazing that our relationships can grow and last! But they can. Especially as we love each other well. And to do that we need to pray like crazy for ourselves, that God will help us as wives to understand our husbands and know what makes them feel loved and respected.

When we love well, we will give our husbands more confidence and belief in themselves, and that will give them confidence and courage as they face their daily battles.

Pray for:

- God to show you how to love well;
- God to convict you of how you're not loving well;

- God to show you how to respect your husband unconditionally;
- God to give you wisdom on how to "speak" love and respect so that your husband hears it;
- wisdom to know when you're trying to show love but it's not coming across that way;
- the ability to truly hear your husband and respond well.

Journal

- What makes you feel loved well? Make a list of at least five things.
- What are the ways you show your husband love? Again, list at least five things.
- Ask your husband, "What makes you feel loved? What do I do that makes you feel respected?"
- Ask God to reveal ways that you are causing your husband to feel disrespected. Make a list. Pray about the list. If appropriate, tell your husband you're sorry. What are ways that you can turn around these situations into showing respect instead?

---

1. Shaunti Feldhahn, *For Women Only: What You Need to Know About the Inner Lives of Men* (Colorado Springs, Colo.: Multnomah Books, 2004), 23.

2. Ibid., 26.

Take Care

I started working out at the gym a couple of months ago. It's something I've wanted to do for a long time and finally got around to. I really don't enjoy exercising. I think it's boring, but I admit it is needed. As I began seeing my body respond, my speed and endurance increase, I became excited. I was proud of my accomplishments. Within two months, I went from doing two fifteen-minute miles to three miles in less than thirty-three minutes.

That's when my knee started hurting.

It began as a hint of pain while pushing hard to finish a mile in under eleven minutes. Then it began hurting even after I had finished exercising. Even hurting a day later. One day after pushing extra hard, I limped up and down the stairs in my office building all day. My knee didn't just hurt; it was painful.

I was pushing too hard.

It was time to back off. To not run every day. To do some strength training and laps in the pool. My knee was telling me in no uncertain terms that I needed to take care of it.

Our bodies have ways of telling us when we need to slow down and take care of ourselves. We begin forgetting things because our brain is on overload. Tears come way too easily because we are emotionally burned out. The end of the day comes, and we want to just collapse and do nothing because we've been doing too much. Our backs ache from the stress buildup. We're surprised at how klutzy we become or how once easy tasks take us forever to complete.

Caregivers need care

As women, we often try to do it all. Work hard at our job.

Rear a family. Be good, loving wives. Get involved in church. Keep our homes neat and clean. Do laundry. Prepare meals. We're created to nurture and encourage, and we take these roles seriously—caring for everyone and everything. Except ourselves.

I cut out and saved a *Sally Forth* comic strip from our Sunday paper. It shows Sally talking to a coworker. The colleague is complaining about her job and how everything she does is for someone else (her boss). Sally asks, "What's your dream?" She replies with a dream from her teenage years, explaining that it's been so long since she thought about her own dreams that she doesn't even know what she'd want.

The comic strip was funny—yet it wasn't. It's true of the lives of way too many wives who give all they have to their jobs and families and have nothing left over at the end of the day.

We need to take care of ourselves—our bodies, our friendships, our dreams, and our relationship with God.

Why include this information in a book about praying for your husbands?

Because taking care of yourself will make you a better wife. Help you be more alert to what to pray for. Allow you to love him better. It may sound a bit crazy, but it's true. You'll have more to give if you take time to recharge and nourish yourself.

What do you need?

So what do you need to do to take care of yourself? What are you missing in your life that will recharge your spirit? What good things do you need to do for yourself?

Sometimes it's even hard to say.

Ask God, "What do I need? What am I not experiencing or doing that You want for me?"

You may be thinking, *So how am I going to fit that into an already too-full schedule?*

Again, pray for wisdom to know what to take off your schedule so that you can do what God truly wants you to do. What on your to-do list is there because you feel you "should" or "no one else will if I don't"? Are there things on your list that God never intended for you to do? If there are, can you take them off? If they don't get done, what's the worst thing that could happen? What's the best thing that could happen? Is it worth trying?

Do you need time with friends? Studies have proven that women who spend time with their friends live longer, healthier lives. The Nurses' Health Study from Harvard Medical School reported that not having friends was as detrimental to health as smoking and carrying extra weight. A 2000 UCLA study on stress and women found that having girlfriends not only helped to lower stress, but lowered blood pressure as well.

Do you need time alone to recharge? I do. I love people—they're one of my passions, and I love spending time with my guys, but I need time alone to recharge. Quiet. Peace. I know this about myself, yet I don't always schedule in alone time because of everything that needs done. Then I wonder why I feel so frazzled.

Be you

Take time to nurture and enjoy things you enjoy. I love reading, so I make time to read good books. Angela enjoys painting and drawing. It relaxes her. Pam likes to get dirty—planting flowers and growing things. It's easy to use up all our time doing things that need done and taking care of others and not do the things that we enjoy doing.

Sometimes when women marry, they put so much energy into making their husbands happy and then their children happy, that they lose themselves. They forget what their hopes and dreams are. They can't remember what they really enjoyed doing because they spend their time doing what others enjoy doing.

Your husband fell in love with you. Don't lose that girl. Take the time to nurture and encourage her. To grow your natural talents. To try new things. A year ago I took an art class at a local gallery and tried a few voice lessons at a music studio. In a couple weeks, I begin a Zumba class. I'm not quite sure what that is, but my friend's son, Dan, tells me it's a lot of fun. So my cousin and I are going to give it a try.

Joining the gym was one of the first things I did for myself in a while. It's been really good for me. Not only physically, but has also built my confidence and belief in myself. My husband has decided to go with me when he can. Today we took a break and went swimming together. As your husband watches you try new things, it may inspire and challenge him to try something new or revive an old hobby himself.

You and God

While spending time with friends, getting exercise, doing things you enjoy, and trying new things are all great ways to take care of you, growing your relationship with God is the most important thing you can do. To really pray like crazy for your husband, you'll need a close relationship with God.

There was a time in my life when I thought that having a close relationship with God meant that I had to get up every morning and spend time studying my Bible and praying, doing things for Him throughout the day, and a list of other things. God finally helped me realize that He didn't want our relationship to be a checklist of things that I thought I had to do and check off. He wanted me. A relationship. He wanted me to just talk to Him. To go for walks with Him. To be aware of His presence throughout my day.

Yes, He did want me to study my Bible, not because I "should" but because I wanted to hear from Him—wanted to know what He was saying to me through it. Yes, He did want me to pray, but not because I had to and not just to ask Him for a list of things, but as a way to know Him and experience Him.

So I pray, like I do for my husband and my kids, that God will help me to know Him as intimately as a human being can know God. And I look for Him throughout my day—in music, in conversations with friends, in the books I choose to read, scripture, work, etc. I talk to Him throughout my day.

Recently, my pastor challenged our team to fast from things that could be taking time away from God or getting in the way of what He wanted for us. One of the things I chose to fast from was listening to the radio on the way to work and instead use that time just to talk to God. It was harder at first than I had imagined. I was so used to flipping on the radio as soon as I came out of the gym. But instead, I began just talking to God about the day ahead while I drove. I thought through the things I needed to accomplish, meetings I would be in, people I would talk to, challenges I faced, and as I thought about them, I talked to God about them (aloud). It was good. It allowed me to spend my early morning time with Him talking about what He was teaching me and about my guys and friends. Now I find myself turning off the radio—on the way to and from work to talk to Him about my day and anything else that is on my heart.

That's what He desires. For us to so want to spend time with Him that we take the initiative because we want to.

And as we spend time with Him, we will naturally grow in Him. Our minds will become more aware of His leading and speaking. About us and about our husbands, enabling us to know how to pray better for both them and ourselves.

Take Care

Praying like crazy can begin only when we're truly taking care of ourselves.

Pray for:

- God to tell you what He wants for you that you're not currently experiencing or doing;
- wisdom to know what to take off your to-do list in order to fit in time to do what God truly wants you to do;
- God to bring godly friends into your life and/or show you who He desires you to build a friendship with;
- you to know God as intimately as a human being can know God;
- Him to make your time with Him special and powerful;
- Him to reveal Himself to you.

Journal

- What are things you enjoyed doing before you were married? Do you still do them now? Why or why not?
- If you had free time and resources, what would you like to do or try? What would it take to do something on your list?
- When do you most feel God's presence? When do you enjoy time with God the most?
- How will you take better care of yourself?

All God Created Them to Be

God has plans, many of them detailed. It always amazes me to learn how complex and interrelated factors make our earth the way we know it—whether it's how the earth spins on its axis or its precise distance from the sun or the impact of one creature on an ecosystem. God has planned this world to work just so.

He also has plans for our spouses. He created our husbands uniquely for a specific purpose. He knew exactly what they would need to influence the world they live in. He gave them gifts and talents, and continues to grow these gifts and talents, for the role He has designed them to play. He created them, planned for them, thinks about them.

> You made all the delicate, inner parts of my body
>   and knit me together in my mother's womb.
> Thank you for making me so wonderfully complex!
>   Your workmanship is marvelous—how well I know it.
> You watched me as I was being formed in utter seclusion,
>   as I was woven together in the dark of the womb.
> You saw me before I was born.
>   Every day of my life was recorded in your book.
> Every moment was laid out
>   before a single day had passed.
> How precious are your thoughts about me, O God.
>   They cannot be numbered!
> I can't even count them;
>   they outnumber the grains of sand! (Psalm
>   139:13–18, NLT).

It's pretty amazing to me. God taking His time to think about and plan each of us individually. Creating us. He didn't just form Adam and Eve and then walk away and say, "OK, whatever happens from here on out, you're on your own." His plans are specific and intentional for each of us.

He thinks about your husband so often, that you can't even count the thoughts. And His thoughts are good. He plans good things.

God has plans

God specifically designed and created your husband with a plan in mind. " 'I know the plans I have for you,' declares the LORD, 'plans to prosper you and not to harm you, plans to give you hope and a future' " (Jeremiah 29:11, NIV).

He designed your husband with unique gifts and talents to use in pursuing those plans. You are the one person to uniquely see what those gifts and talents are. Others may get glimpses from their perspectives, but you see what others don't.

What can you do to encourage your husband and his gifts, talents, and passions? Ask God to show you. Ask your husband for ideas. Affirm what you see God doing in his life and how He has gifted him.

I recognized long before anyone else did—including Tim—what an amazing voice he has. (I heard him singing around the house, singing in the car, and singing next to me at church.) He loves music. His tastes have changed through the years, but music has always been a big part of his life. But he never sang—not by himself in public.

So for his fortieth birthday, I gave him voice lessons as a gift. I paid for one month, not sure he'd take that many lessons. He continued for years—until his voice teacher retired. He has attended music schools in Nashville and has sung at churches across Pennsylvania—and even in Australia. I believe God has specifically gifted him for a purpose and have looked for ways to encourage, affirm, and support that gift. I've prayed and asked God to give him the opportunities to use his voice, to open doors for him, and to help him to believe in whatever plans God has for him through music.

It doesn't always happen

Unfortunately, with the entrance of sin, things don't always go according to God's plans. Sin affects everything. Mentally, physically, emotionally, spiritually. Not just our sin, but other people's sin and just living in a sinful world.

A drunk driver causes an accident that takes away a young man's ability to walk. Someone else's choices forever impact another person's life.

The diagnosis is cancer and the prognosis isn't good. Our sinful world has weakened our bodies physically and allowed diseases that God didn't create.

A father withholds love and speaks only critical, destructive words; and a boy's confidence and life is forever damaged. He may grow up not knowing how to really love his own wife and children, never fully believing in himself, never trusting the people around him. God intended him to grow up to be loved, valued, and accepted—enabling him to be all he was created to be, but his emotional wounds get in the way.

A young person makes choices, feeling invincible, that forever affect his life. A little peer pressure, the desire to have fun, and he is addicted to drugs. It will become the addiction he fights most of his life, sometimes causing him to make other choices in order to feed his need. Twenty years later, he looks back at years of destruction and a wasted life.

Whether it's someone else's choice, our choice, or just the sinful world we live in, life can be hard and often takes turns that we never expected—or wanted. We have an enemy who is out to destroy us. An enemy who wants nothing more than to keep us from being all God created us to be.

God never gives up

But God never gives up. No matter what our choices, no matter what happens in our lives, He is there and is willing to redeem that life. To turn it around for good. He doesn't want to just "make it better," but, if allowed, will use it for something tremendous.

Joseph experienced evil transformed into good. His life took a twist he never expected as the result of jealous brothers. Yet years later he was able to say, "Don't you see, you planned evil against me but God used those same plans for my good" (Genesis 50:20, *The Message*).

The Bible promises "that God causes everything to work together for the good of those who love God and are called according to his purpose for them" (Romans 8:28, NLT).

God plans that no matter what happens in our lives, He will turn it around for good, use it for our good—and often the good of others.

So God created our husbands with a plan and also planned to redeem everything that happens in their lives for good in order to accomplish His plan for them. He will use everything that happens in their lives to enable them to be the men He created them to be. And we wives are a part of that plan.

Joining God

We can join God in helping our husbands be all God created them to be by praying for it. By asking God to do what it takes to enable them to be the men He created them to be. This enabling may require healing of past wounds and choices. They might need to forgive themselves or others. It will most likely require courage and strength. It may mean that they just need to figure out what God has created them for and do it. Or even to believe that God has something for them in the first place.

Ask God to open your husband's eyes to the possibilities—for him to see what God has created him to do. Pray that God will give him the courage to follow those plans. Ask God to give your husband purpose and passion. Pray that God will overcome any obstacle, hurt, wound, or anything else the devil has put in the way to thwart God's plan.

As I type these words, my husband is planning for college. He never intended to begin college at fifty. (He never intended to attend college at all!) But classes begin in two weeks.

After thirty years with one company, working in a specialized job that didn't easily transfer outside that industry, Tim found himself needing a new plan. He'd intended to stay at the company for the rest of his working life. He enjoyed his job and enjoyed the team of people he worked with. It was a good fit for his personality and talents. He really didn't know what he wanted to do next. Where do you begin when you need to re-create yourself?

I began praying. I believed God had a plan. That He had something special for Tim. I believed that God had a purpose for Tim and that this was an opportunity for Tim to pursue it.

I asked God to guide him and to show him what He created him to do. I asked God to show Tim that this was a God-opportunity—that God had a plan and it would be good. I assured my husband that a few years down the road, he'd look back and say, "Wow, God had good plans. I'm glad for it! I feel like what I am doing now is what I was born to do!" I encouraged Tim to look for ways to use his talents and passions for God.

I asked God to give Tim the courage to step out and do something he was passionate about or at the least, interested in, and asked God to prevent him from taking just any job. I believed God was in this. That He had a plan. That He had created Tim for something more.

So in two weeks, Tim will be taking classes, doing homework, and following God's plan for his life, trusting God to lead and guide and courageously believing that it will be good.

Supporting role

While I am an optimist and I think Tim's going to love school, and it will be exciting and better than he anticipates, I'm a realist. I know that there will be changes in our lives as a result. I know that it will be hard and that he'll have to learn to study again. His schedule will be crazy with early classes some days and late classes others. When he's home, he will need to focus and study.

So I'm already praying.

I'm asking God to give Tim everything he needs to follow His plan. Whether it's resources or attitude, that God will guide and be evident. That God will encourage him along the way and affirm that this is what God has for him.

I know there will be moments when the devil will attempt to thwart God's plan. He will whisper to Tim that it's too hard or attempt to overwhelm him or get him to quit. He desires for Tim to not believe in himself enough, to doubt the plans and to not take the risk and follow through.

I am praying that God will bind the devil. That God will speak words of courage all along the way and help Tim to know the truth.

I am also asking God to show me how to best support Tim. There is more to supporting him than just prayer. I need to put action to my words.

It will mean giving him the time he needs to work on his schoolwork—even if I would rather that he spend time with me. To counter the lies of the devil, I will need to be intentional about speaking words of encouragement and belief. I'm already working on it. Telling him he can do this. That he has what it takes. Reminding him that I believe in him. Asking God to prompt me to say the things Tim needs to hear.

As wives, we can daily ask God, "How can I best support my husband today as he attempts to be all You created him to be? As he follows Your plan for his life?"

We can also ask our husbands, "Honey, how can I be supportive of you? What can I do to help? Are there things I can specifically pray for?" One of the things Tim asked me to do early on is not to share ideas with him. I am an idea person. They just pop into my head one right after another. When I see a challenge or a problem, I quickly have several ideas for getting through it. Tim is going back to school; I may just have an idea or two of what he could do or how he could do it. One of the ways I need to be supportive of his process is to keep my ideas to myself. So I'm trying. And I gave him permission to tell me, "No thank you, I really don't want to hear your idea right now."

Getting in the way

Sometimes one of the most supportive things we can do is to get out of the way. The devil will use any means he can to keep our husbands from being the men God created them to be. Sometimes God uses us. But sometimes we may be holding our husbands back from God's plans.

When Karen's husband wanted to go back to school and change careers, she said No. Their family was young. It would mean a few years of financial challenges. It would cause him to be away from home more as he balanced work by day and school by night. She didn't want to pay the price. So Harold packed up his passion and excitement and dreams and stuck with the job he didn't really love. He's provided well for his family. But what could life have been like if he had followed his passions? What if that was what God had created him to do?

Jerry knows God has called him to minister to the teenagers on his block. Once a week, they gather in his driveway to play basketball. Afterward they head inside to eat pizza and just hang out. He wants to make himself available to the boys. It amazes him that something as simple as throwing a ball around and offering a little food causes the boys to trust him and open up to him. They call him when they're struggling. Stop by when they need someone to talk to or to share a success. Paige believes that God is using Jerry to influence the boys and knows that he sets boundaries around family time—putting her and their grown children first. But sometimes she gets irritated at the interruptions. And even though Jerry cleans up the kitchen after the boys leave, she gets annoyed that they're hanging out in her kitchen in the first place. She tries to hide her frustrations, but Jerry can tell by the way she withdraws from him. Hides upstairs reading while the boys are downstairs. Is silent for a few hours afterward. He wants to make her happy and wants to do what God has called him to do, and he's torn between the influence he has in the lives of the boys and the unhappiness of his wife.

Kerry doesn't know how much longer he can keep it up. Working his day job and then putting time and energy into building his own business at night, while trying to keep up with the demands of home and family. How does a guy do it all? Sheila agreed that this is what God wanted. They had prayed together and separately about it and felt God leading. But no matter how many hours he puts into the job and the business, she has a honey-do list waiting for him when he gets home. He's exhausted. He believes this is God's will, but how does he keep it all going?

Praying Like Crazy for Your Husband

Whether intentionally or unintentionally, wives sometimes hold their husbands back.

It may be out of fear—we're comfortable with the way things are and are afraid of change. Karen loves Harold and would never want to hold him back from what God was calling him to do, but she also didn't want to give up their comfortable life or have him away from home in the evenings. She was afraid of how difficult it would make their lives and just wasn't willing to risk it.

While Paige saw God working and believed Jerry was following God's plan, she didn't want to get involved and was often jealous of the connection Jerry had with the boys. He was doing everything he could to put her first and she would never criticize him, but her silences spoke volumes.

Sheila believed God was leading Kerry to start the new business, but she still expected him to keep up with everything she wanted him to do at home, not realizing that her expectations were causing him to consider giving up. She wanted God's will, but wanted Kerry to do everything she wanted him to do as well.

Without realizing it, a wife can become jealous of what is happening in her husband's life and thus sabotage his successes with criticisms or negative comments. She may express her resentment in silences that go on for days or in negative comments to others. Whether or not he hears the comments, her attitude undermines what God is doing in and through his life. We wives can speak a lack of support and unbelief through words, actions, and silence.

Pray and ask God to show you if there are ways you might be preventing your husband from being all God created him to be. Are you holding him back by a lack of support? Out of your own fear? Or an unwillingness to go through a little discomfort in order for him to transition to where God wants him? Are you jealous or possibly competing with him? Confess anything God brings to your mind. Then ask God to change you. To give you peace, courage—whatever you need in order to fully support your husband.

The men we want them to be

Sometimes we are really more interested in our husbands becoming the men we want them to be than becoming the people God created them to be. We want to change them. We have convinced ourselves that the change is for the best—they'll be a better person. And often we try to do the "changing" ourselves—using nagging, criticisms, buying the "right" clothes for them, etc.

Perhaps he's quiet, but we think he should be more outgoing. He likes his time alone, but we want him to spend his time with people. He loves to tell stories, but we feel he should ask more questions and listen more. He's practical; we want him to be romantic. He's spontaneous; we want him to plan things in advance.

We forget that God has designed and created him specifically—given him the personality styles and traits and characteristics that are uniquely his for a reason. We cannot change a quiet guy into a gregarious guy or change a loner to a party animal. God may have given him a gift for storytelling that reaches people better than if he tried to figure out questions to ask.

This can be hard, but we need to ask God to show us the ways we're trying to change our husbands and then leave the changing up to the Holy Spirit. Give it to God. Tell Him alone what you want, but surrender that desire to God's will. Ask God to help you accept your husband the way God created him—to see the positive and blessing in him.

Praying Like Crazy for Your Husband

Tim and I are opposites. I love a good book. He is not into reading, though he can listen to books on his iPod while walking and working around the house. I would have company over every weekend. He prefers it to be just the two of us. He's more guarded and reserved. I typically talk easily and openly. He researches and thinks before making any decision. I make decisions sometimes with little thought at all. I just "feel" that this is the right decision. He likes to save and scrimp, skipping purchasing things because we can. While I like to save and not have debt, I also like to spend a little here and there on what could be deemed as nonessentials, such as new clothes, eating out, a new book or CD. (Admittedly, we drive each other crazy sometimes!)

Yet I've learned to appreciate what makes Tim, Tim. Prayer helps. Asking God to help me see Tim as He sees him. Talking to God about the ways Tim drives me crazy at times. And learning to see the positive in who he is. His penny pinching has left us in a good place financially, despite losing his job. He has taught me to enjoy the outdoors and appreciate being alone. (Now I'm the one who craves it!) I know when he makes a decision it will be a good, well-thought-out decision. Recognizing that God created Tim to be this person I'm married to for a reason, reminds me that part of that reason may be to balance *me* and help *me* to grow.

It may be hard, but God can help us surrender what we want him to be like and learn to prefer the man God created him to be.

He needs you

God knew your husband would need you in order to be all He created your husband to be. He saw it from the very beginning. When He created Adam, He saw that Adam needed Eve. The Bible calls her his *ezer knegdo. Ezer* is a name used for God in stories where someone desperately needed His help. *Knegdo* basically means "like to himself"—a partner, a helper that suited him. Adam wasn't complete without Eve. He needed her in order to live the life God planned for him. Your husband desperately needs you in order to be the man God has called him to be. He needs your support, your encouragement, and your prayers.

Pray for:

- God to enable your husband to be all He created him to be;
- God to open your husband's eyes to the plans He has for him and for the courage to follow those plans;
- God to provide all your husband's needs to follow God's plan;
- God to encourage him along the way;
- God to affirm that these are the plans He has for him;
- God to show you how to be supportive;
- God to give you the words to say to support and encourage your husband;
- God to help you not to hold him back in any way;
- God to show you if there are ways—fear, not wanting change, etc.—that you might be preventing him from being all God created him to be;
- forgiveness and ask God to change you if needed;
- God to show you if there are ways you're attempting to make your husband into what you want instead of what God desires;
- the peace to accept the man God has created your husband to be—quirks and all.

Journal

- What are the unique gifts and passions God has given your husband? Make a list.
- How do you see God using your husband?
- How can you be supportive to your husband as he follows God's plans?
- Are there ways you are showing a lack of support for your husband? Are there things you need to change?

Jobs

Tim and I met at work. We dated for more than two years before we were married. Our coworkers threw us a bridal shower and attended our wedding. Three years later, they celebrated the birth of our first son, Josh, with a baby shower and a farewell party for me. I left the company to stay home with our son while Tim continued on—changing departments and jobs within the organization for thirty years.

Some of the changes were good. Jobs Tim enjoyed and excelled in. Others were more difficult. Challenging bosses or tasks. As the years passed, I knew fewer and fewer of his colleagues. Many I had worked with transferred or moved away, or Tim changed to a department in which I didn't know anyone. But one thing remained consistent from the beginning. My prayers for his job.

Work is often the place our husbands spend most of their time. It's possible that they will spend more time with coworkers, clients, or customers than they will at home with the family. Their lives (and ours) will be greatly affected by their job, their boss, and everything else that's a part of their day. And the reverse is true, as well; they have the opportunity to influence those they work with or serve. So work is an important topic to pray for.

Much to pray for

There's much to pray for in regard to our husbands' jobs. If they work for other people, we can pray for their bosses and colleagues—that they will see our husbands as God desires and that He will influence these coworkers through our husbands. The workplace may be filled with people looking for hope and courage, who are struggling but don't know God. Our husbands can be witnesses in their company or department.

Praying Like Crazy for Your Husband

I have prayed that Tim's bosses will see the man of integrity that he is and that they will recognize the energy and effort he puts into his work. Tim is a perfectionist and works hard to do his job to the best of his ability. I've also prayed that God will bless him with good working relationships with his coworkers and those that he has supervised. It's always been fun to go to Christmas parties or other work-related gatherings and hear how men who worked for Tim talked to him and about him and see the respect they have for him.

If your husband is the owner of a business or is a supervisor, then praying for his leadership and the way he treats others is important. Also pray that God will send the right employees for the company who will work with integrity and be a good reflection of the company.

Besides relationships on the job, there is the daily grind of getting work done, projects that need to be completed, angry customers, safety, changes, etc. Listen as your husband talks about work; look for things to pray about. Ask him, "What can I be praying about for your job?"

Often as wives, we know the challenges our husbands are facing on the job. The pending project, irate customer, demanding boss, a job he just doesn't like, and the temptations he will face each day.

Depending on his job, personality, coworkers, and job location, our husbands will face temptations. There may be a coworker who flirts and teases and makes it clear she's interested in a little fun. He may have unlimited access to finances and could easily alter the books. Travel may take him to places where no one knows his name or would know or care what he does while he is there. His buddies may invite him to the bar after work to unwind before heading home. He may work with a female coworker on many projects, building a relationship that grows into a friendship where they begin to share on a level outside of just work, never intentionally planning on anything happening but work, until they realize that they are emotionally attached to each other. The devil will look for ways to tempt him and draw him away from God and his family—and to ruin his reputation and self-esteem as well. This is an area that needs prayer. We can fight the battle with our husbands by daily praying for the temptations they face—for the known ones they share or just for a hedge of protection from whatever they're facing.

This is important. Because they spend so much time at work, they will most likely face more temptations at work than just about anywhere else. And it's an area in which many men think they're safe and they fall. Most of us know stories of men who have had affairs with coworkers (even men who are working in ministry) or who have been caught embezzling from the company or just wanted to unwind with the guys and instead found themselves drinking and then driving and ending up in an accident—sometimes where someone else is hurt.

We can help protect our husbands and help them face the temptations victoriously by praying with them and for them. Ecclesiastes challenges, "Two people are better off than one, for they can help each other succeed. If one person falls, the other can reach out and help. But someone who falls alone is in real trouble" (Ecclesiastes 4:9, 10, NLT). We don't want to leave our husbands alone without prayer support in the workplace. We can help them succeed by praying.

When there is no job

We knew the meeting was important. We learned about it when we returned from vacation. It was scheduled for that Thursday. The entire department of more than a dozen men who had worked most of their lives for the company was asked to attend. While everyone knew it was a possibility, no one really expected it. But it was true. The company was closing down the department and letting all of them go.

Everything about our life changed that day. Tim had been there for thirty years. It was all he knew. He had provided well for us through his work, but his job was very specific to the industry. What would he do now? He enjoyed his job and excelled at it. He really didn't want to change careers. But he had no choice. He also had no real idea of what he wanted to do because he had never given it much thought. Why think about a new career when you enjoy the one you have so much?

Tim's story isn't unusual. In the past two years, half the men in our family have lost their jobs. Finding new ones hasn't happened quickly. Most have been unemployed for months before finding work. Others have been out of work for a year or more. Several have gone back to school in order to build new careers. That's where Tim is. At a time of life where we thought we'd be slowing down, enjoying fewer bills now that our sons are grown and out of school, he's back in school, spending most of his waking moments studying, going to classes, and working on projects.

When our husbands lose their jobs, the trauma includes more than simply not being employed and needing to find work. While we will pray for the right new job for them and God's leading and purpose, so much else is going on inside. A man's sense of identity is connected to his job. All too often, loss of a job includes loss of his identity and his main source of value and security. We may need to pray that God will help him find his security and value in Christ alone and to help him see that he is more than a job. A husband may also struggle with feeling he's letting his family down because he's not providing for them financially. The rejection he experiences when prospective employers either say, "No, thank you" or they don't call back, can be hard to handle over and over again.

After a job loss, it's not unusual for some men to experience depression or to "hide out" at home—not risking rejection by not looking for a job. They may withdraw from the family, despite having more time on their hands.

It's a time when wives need to pray—not only for new jobs but for everything our husbands are dealing with: protection from depression, acknowledgment of their value in Christ, recognition of their importance to the family outside of money, courage to look for a job, peace about rejection, and the ability to see this as a God-possibility. From the beginning of this journey, I've told Tim that this situation is a God-possibility. I've reminded him that his layoff didn't catch God by surprise and that God has a plan that will be better than what Tim had at his old job.

It's also a time when we need to pray for ourselves. Our lives have changed as well. Our husbands are now home full time. They're dealing with a lot of different things. Money may be tighter, so the budget may need to be cut. And we may need to either go back to work or work more. Tim and I were lucky in that my company actually needed me to go full time to pick up some extra projects and then kept me full time after those projects were completed. But it's been an adjustment for me to work a full-time job that is often much more than just full time.

We wives may also be dealing with our own attitudes and feelings toward our husbands. We may be angry at them for losing their job if it was as a result of something they did. We may struggle to respect them when they don't look for jobs or don't look as hard as we think they should. We may become frustrated that they're always around and we no longer have time to ourselves. Tim worked out of a home office for the last year of his job, so I was used to his being home most days, but he also traveled a couple days a week. Having him home every day was a big adjustment for me because I like having the house to myself—alone time is how I recharge.

We can take each of these challenges to God, allowing Him to not only work in our husbands but in us wives as well. Asking Him to give us wisdom in what to say and what not to say, asking Him to help us to not nag, but to be a source of encouragement to our husbands, while at the same time, not enabling them to sit home and sulk.

Remember to say Thank You

Prayer isn't always asking. We need to remember to be thankful. A good job and a hardworking husband are two things to be very thankful for. Don't forget to thank God for the ways He provides for your husband and for your family through his job. Not only financially, but simple things such as the opportunity to help a customer in a special way, the joy of being able to witness to a coworker going through a hard time, a good boss, a project completed, opportunities to grow and be challenged, and any way that you see God working in and through your husband as a result of his job.

It's also nice to say Thank you to our husbands for working and providing for us. Yes, I realize that in most homes, wives are working and providing as well. Wouldn't it be nice for us to hear our husbands thank us for the effort? Thank us for being dependable and hard working? Our husbands would appreciate hearing these words as well. Sincere and without strings—so if they say Thank you back, great, but if not, that's OK too. We can help encourage and build up our husbands as we show respect for what they do to take care of our families.

Pray for:

- his boss, coworkers, clients, and customers—that they will have a positive impact on your husband and your husband will influence them;
- specific challenges you know your husband is facing;
- your husband to be able to face changes at work well;

- God to protect him from the temptations he faces in his work;
- God to protect his reputation and allow others to see your husband as God wants them to;
- a new job, if necessary;
- his attitude as he struggles through things at work or with unemployment;
- a thankful heart—to God for the job and for your husband as well.

Journal

- What do you appreciate about your husband in relationship to his job, the way he works, and/or the way he provides for your family? Make a list. Verbally thank him for some of the things on your list.
- Are there challenges or temptations you know your husband faces at work? How can you best support him in this area?
- What are specifics you know your husband would appreciate you praying for in regard to his job?

Parenting

The picture of Tim holding our new baby, with the hospital window lighting father and son, is one of my favorite pictures from Josh's birth. A younger version of my husband holding our sleeping baby, a slight smile on his face as he gazes on this tiny infant. Josh appears to be sleeping contentedly with one small hand and his long fingers sticking out from under the blue blanket, the hospital cap covering the dark hair he inherited from both of us.

Almost three years later, we welcomed Zachary into the world on a sunshiny Friday afternoon. Unlike his quieter brother, Zachary came into the world with his eyes and mouth wide open. The two have been different ever since.

So have our lives.

Becoming a parent changes your life. It also changes our prayers for our husbands as we add praying for them as a father.

Being a daddy

I asked Tim, "What was the biggest change in your life when you became a new dad?"

"I no longer wanted to walk on telephone lines thirty feet in the air," he replied. When Josh was born, Tim was a service technician for a company that required him often to work (not walk, but he liked adventure) on lines strung on telephone poles. He continued to explain that being a dad created a new sense of responsibility. "Something changes in your thinking, and you no longer want to take needless risks because you have a baby at home depending on you."

As our husbands become daddies, the number one thing we can pray for is wisdom—that God will give them wisdom in raising these little ones who they are now responsible for. Tim said this would be the number one thing he wanted me to pray about for him as a father.

Beyond wisdom, I have also always prayed for Tim's relationship with our sons, asking God to bind them close, to show them how to truly love and care about one another. I've prayed that Tim would see each son as God sees him and have wisdom to know how to parent them individually—what worked for one did not always work for the other. As in most homes, our sons were very different from one other. While what they needed from Tim as a father was basically the same (learning how to be godly, responsible men), *how* they received that from Tim needed to be different. I've prayed that Tim will see their differences, see what works with each one, and be able to parent in the most effective ways.

Parenting biological children is different from parenting stepchildren. Parenting kids who live with you is different from parenting children who live with another parent in a different house. There will be challenges when children have more than one dad or mom. Challenges when children live in two different locations. Dads need prayers for each of these unique parenting roles, especially for wisdom, as they attempt to influence, love, and rear all of their children.

Wives and moms will know the specific challenges our husbands face as fathers and can lift each of these specific things to God—whether it's being a stepdad or parenting kids who live in a different house, relating to a little girl, dealing with a teenager's attitude, learning how to control his anger, or whatever is unique to your home. God will give you specific insights into how to pray for your husband and his role of parenting. And when we don't know how to pray for them, we can ask God, "I don't know how to pray for him as a father. Please show me how to pray."

Growing from a daddy to a dad

When they were little, the boys loved to play hide-and-seek with their dad in the evenings. We didn't have television for much of their growing-up years, so evenings found us entertaining our sons by playing games and reading books. Josh and Zach would find a place to hide together. It was never really a secret where they were; you could hear them giggling and talking. Daddy would make a big deal, talking loudly about trying to find them—"Where can they be?"—making them giggle even louder. Lots of laughter when they were finally found.

Then it would be Tim's turn to hide. The house was typically dark (except for the light I was using to read—my time to sit and relax). The boys would hunt nervously and excitedly—knowing what would happen when they finally found Daddy. Slowly peaking behind doors and in the shower, they would let out screams and then lots of laughter as Daddy revealed his hiding place with a yell. We called it hide-and-seek-and-scare.

As the boys grew, they went from calling Tim "Daddy" to "Dad," and the things they did together changed as well. No more hide-and-seek. Instead they went for bike rides, camping, and hiking.

As their relationship changed, I prayed that God would give Tim wisdom on how to change the way he parented as well. When they're little, there's a lot more telling them what to do. As they grow older, we begin to coach them more, asking questions and helping them make their own decisions with guidance, always retaining the authority to overrule their choice. As they move into adulthood, the relationship changes again, with Tim becoming friend and occasional advisor.

The transition isn't always easy. How do you know when to transition? Is there a certain age when you stop telling and start guiding and allowing them to make more and more decisions? Is there a time when you stop telling and just enjoy a relationship with your adult child?

I've asked God to help Tim with the answers to these questions—that God would show him how to parent at each stage and age.

For some parents, the various parenting stages will be harder. Some fathers may want to be their child's friend from day one and struggle with guiding and telling. Other dads may never want to stop telling; they may not know what parenting looks like if they aren't disciplining and making decisions for their children—or at least helping with decision making even when not asked.

How we parent is definitely influenced by the type of parenting we had. But God can grow us, teach us, and change us. So I prayed that God would give Tim the tools and desires he needed to parent through the various stages. And now that our sons are adults, I pray that Tim will enjoy a new relationship with his sons, enjoy hanging out with them and talking to them.

A godly man

Tim says the most challenging aspect of being a dad is being a spiritual leader—knowing how to raise children who love God, have an intimate relationship with Him, and want to walk in His ways. Beyond reading a devotional for family worship, praying together before meals, and going to church as a family, Tim has wanted to show what it means to walk with God obediently, to make decisions based on what God wants, and to serve Him in all areas.

That's a huge challenge.

I've heard several men share that when something is really hard and they're not sure what to do, they will often not do anything instead of doing something and failing. They don't want to fail, so they'll just not attempt something in order to not fail at it. Could this be one reason many dads do little, even though they acknowledge they should be the spiritual leaders of their home? Many moms complain that their husbands aren't more involved in family worship or teaching their children about God. Is it possible they just don't know how? This is something wives can definitely pray about.

Pray that God will not only give your husband wisdom in how to be the spiritual leader of your home, but that God will deepen your husband's relationship with Him. As we walk closely with God and learn more of Him and His love for us, we will naturally share Christ more with others. Ask God to open your husband's eyes to how He's working in his life, to reveal how much He loves him, and to help Him to know God as intimately as a human being can know God.

God can and will give fathers ideas and opportunities to show their children how to walk with Him. It may be through family worship, but it may be by teaching their kids about nature and showing them God through the outdoors. Or helping them see God through art or music or books. Our husbands may have a knack for making the Bible truths simple or turn everyday experiences into spiritual lessons.

Often we think that being the spiritual leader of a home means leading family worship. But being the spiritual leader is more than that. It is fighting the spiritual battle in prayer for his family, living a godly example, revealing an example of God's love in the way he loves his children, and making God real in his own unique way. God will blend the husband's and wife's uniqueness into a team that shares God with their family.

When our sons were growing up, I was great at reading books and coming up with creative family worship ideas, but I knew little about nature. Tim grew up loving the outdoors. He passed on his love for nature and God together by taking our boys (and me) to Yosemite, the Rocky Mountains, the Smoky Mountains, Maine, and anywhere else we could hike, canoe, or mountain bike. I am grateful Tim could show them this side of God.

As wives, we can encourage our husbands in the ways they show our children God while not berating them for not doing it the way we think they should. Each of us has our own unique ways of experiencing God, and we will teach our children from those ways. Tim has taught our boys about God through nature and music; I've shown them God through books and activities. Neither is right or wrong; both are needed. We can work together and complement each other as we raise godly children.

Daddy, play ball with me

Our lives are so busy today. We're working more hours than a decade ago. We're involved in more activities than a generation ago. Technology that was supposed to make our lives easier has actually made us busier—giving us more distractions and things to do. Sometimes our busyness takes us away from the things that are most important, like spending time with our children.

Some men are great at engaging with their children. Playing ball, talking, building projects together, helping with homework. Other fathers may lack the role models or tools for knowing how to engage with their children—not only spending time playing with them, but listening, hearing, really seeing and knowing their kids.

If this is a challenge our husbands face, we can pray that God will show them how to engage, give them a desire to connect with their kids, and help them to really see and hear their children. Ask God to help your husband make the time to do things with the family or with each individually. We will never *find* the time, but we can *make* the time. God may begin by giving them the desire to make the time.

Josh and Zach always enjoyed their monthly "dates" with Dad when they were younger. It was never anything big. Breakfast at the diner nearby. Grilled cheese sandwiches after a bike ride. Their turns alternated each month, and they always knew whose turn it was. Those dates were special, but they were also a challenge. The enemy doesn't want fathers and sons or daughters connecting. He knows how important Dad is in his children's lives and will do all he can to keep it from happening. Busyness may seem like an innocent and unpreventable obstacle, but it may also be the enemy keeping dads from really knowing their kids.

Children need to know Dad loves them, cares about them, and believes in them. Without such assurance, kids grow into adults who are wounded or unsure of themselves. They need Dad not only when they're young, but especially as they grow into teenagers and face new temptations and challenges. It's a time of life when peers often try to persuade them that parents don't know anything and don't really care. And often a time of life when dads start backing off a bit, feeling pushed out and unsure of what to do. We can pray that God will help them to engage with our children no matter what their age and even more so as the kids grow older. Even now that our sons are grown, I pray that God will help Tim to connect with his sons, call them, e-mail them, invite them to do things together, and continue to show that he cares about them.

As we pray for our husbands and their role and influence as fathers, we are, in essence, fighting for our children as well. It's more than just Dad and kids getting along or having fun together. Kids need their dads to help them know that they have what it takes to be an adult. They need to know that Dad loves them and believes they can do it.

Moms are important, but are often taken for granted. Kids are often confident that Mom is there and cares. Children sometimes aren't always as sure of Dad. Josh once said, "Moms love you no matter what, even if you're ax murderers. But Dads are different." Kids need more than Mom's love and attention; they need Dad's too. The devil will attempt to keep Dad busy and distracted or constantly make sure that Dad gets the message that he doesn't know what he's doing as a dad and doesn't have what it takes, either way, causing dads to not engage with their children. It's an area we moms need to cover in prayer—fighting for our children and our husbands.

When it's not a happy, happy home

On television, families face challenges, parents handle them with humor and wisdom, and everything ends happily ever after. Cliff Huxtable, John Walton, and Ward Cleaver faced the challenges of parenting and had children who loved them and respected them.

But not all our families are happy. Dads don't always handle every situation well. Some fathers may not handle any situation well. How do we pray for our husbands as fathers in the midst of anger and wounded relationships? What do we do when Dad and kids don't talk to each other or talk unkindly about each other? It's hard living in a house when people aren't talking to each other, doors are slamming, or worse.

Women often want to fix the problems. Defend Dad to the kids, the kids to Dad. We may battle our own anger and frustration with how things are being handled—we may be angry at our husbands for not parenting the way we think they should or for not parenting well. We may not agree with what they're doing. (If husbands are verbally, physically, or emotionally abusive, we must protect our children and get them help.)

These are situations that demand prayer. We cannot fix things. We can try and try, but only God can truly heal wounds, convict people of wrong, and lead people to do what's right. Again, we can fight for both our husband and our children on our knees, by praying specifically and asking God to intervene—to convict our husbands and our children of wrong and reveal what they should be doing instead. We can pray that God will give our husbands wisdom in healing the relationship, asking God to soften hearts, to give each of them a desire for healing, and the words and actions needed to work toward that healing.

We also need to pray for ourselves, especially if we're angry at our husbands. Tell God what you're thinking and feeling (He already knows) and ask Him to give you the attitude He wants you to have. Pray that He will give you wisdom in what to say or do, or the peace to remain silent.

As we intercede for our families, God will work. He will bring healing, wisdom, and courage. Pray for hearts to be open to His leading. Thank Him for what He's doing, even when you can't see Him at work. Thanking Him anyway will bring you more courage and peace in believing that He is at work even if you don't see progress. Trust Him to know what has to happen to bring real healing and not just surface healing.

The joy of being a dad

I asked Tim what the most rewarding thing about being a parent has been for him. "Watching them grow and learn and discover things," he said.

Parenting changes with each stage of our kids' growth. From infants to toddlers to the "why?" stage to elementary school, puppy love, crushes, heart breaks, the first car, the first job, graduation, college, and marriage, we have the privilege of watching and influencing our children. We can pray that God will help our husbands find joy in each stage, be engaged throughout their children's lives, and reveal God to them in ways only fathers can.

Pray for:

- his relationship with each of his children;

- his role as a stepparent;
- specific challenges you see/know;
- him to engage with his children;
- wisdom;
- his relationship to grow and change as the children grow;
- him to be the spiritual leader his children need;
- his relationship with God;
- healing for his relationships, if needed.

Journal

- What's one of your favorite memories of your husband in his role of Dad to your kids?
- What is your greatest burden for him as a parent?
- What are your husband's best qualities as a dad? Make a list. Affirm him for these.
- What areas challenge him most as a dad? Make a list and pray for him in these areas.

He's Someone's Little Boy

I still sometimes introduce Zachary as "my baby." He's a handsome, grown man, who works six days a week and has grown-up "toys." But to me, he will always be my baby—that cute curious little boy with the dimples when he smiles and the baseball cap on crooked. (He no longer wears the baseball cap.) My mom still refers to my brothers as "the boys," even though they are men approaching fifty who have raised their families and are welcoming their own grandchildren.

No matter how old they are or what they've accomplished, our husbands will always be someone's little boy.

It's a relationship that influences not only who they were and their history, but also their daily life and the person they are. It may be a positive relationship that has helped them to become strong, caring men who have seen modeled how to love a family well. But parents can also damage and wound their children by their actions and words or by their neglect—both physical and emotional. And sometimes even after little boys have grown and left the home, parents can sometimes continue to demand much from their sons.

Their family heritage is a part of who our husbands were and are, and this heritage affects our lives in ways we recognize—and in ways we don't even think about or realize. We may see the effect of visits and phone calls today, but we may not recognize the impact of the lessons taught and the "voice" of their parent continuing in their head. Our parents have played—or failed to play—the most important role in our lives before we are married.

It may not be an area we've thought to pray about often. Yet there is so much to pray like crazy about.

Your mom and dad

If we've prayed for our husbands and their parents, the most obvious thing we may be praying about is for their current relationship with their mom and dad. And that's important.

I have often prayed for Tim to make the time and have the idea to visit with his parents, to call them, to show them honor and value by giving them time and attention. I know how much I enjoy and appreciate a visit with one of my sons—even if it's just a phone call visit. Joshua lives four hours away in another state. I know he lives a busy life. So when he calls, I feel honored that he would set aside time, knowing that our phone calls tend to go on a bit, making the effort to connect with me. Yesterday afternoon I was just sitting down to dinner in a restaurant on the other side of the country from my home when my phone rang. It was Josh. He didn't know I was out of town for work and just decided to call. Instead of eating all by myself, I enjoyed dinner "with" him, as he talked and caught me up on what was happening in his life. I saw his phone call as a gift—from Josh and from God.

Our lives can become so busy and full, that we forget or put off making that phone call or visiting our parents. So it's an area that I've prayed about for Tim, that God would help him continue to build and keep that relationship with his parents, sharing his life, caring about theirs.

For some, this may be a no-brainer. They may have grown up in a close, loving family; and staying in touch with their parents is natural. Others may have had a close, loving family, but find it a bit tougher to think about phoning or visiting or doing things with their parents still. Too many other things and people vie for their attention. We have our own families to take care of—school, soccer practice, youth group, etc. We may live miles apart. And for others, family wasn't a loving, caring place, and they'd rather forget then go back.

Even within the same family, some may be great at continuing that relationship, and others may not. My brother Darren calls my mom twice a week like clockwork on his way home from work. It means a lot to her. She reminds me often (I don't call like clockwork) that Darren calls on Mondays and Thursdays. My brother Nile may not call twice a week, but he stops by at least once a week to see if there's anything she needs. He makes sure repairs are made and the grass is mowed. Each has his own way of staying in touch.

It's a tricky thing. Some parents would love to hear a bit more from their kids. Other parents may still have too much influence on their sons, demanding much. And some husbands may still be too tied to Mama's apron strings, calling Mom to find out what her opinion or thought is, what she recommends, instead of leaving and cleaving to his wife. Other parents have so wounded their children that even though there is no relationship now, the damage continues to affect their sons and, in turn, their families.

So we begin by praying for the relationship and the specific needs or challenges we see. Again, as wives, God has given us a front-row seat to our husbands and what happens not only in their lives, but often in their hearts. This allows us to know how to pray for them like no one else in their lives can.

How is your husband's relationship with his parents? Is it strong? Does he need to do a better job at staying in touch? Does he need to cut the apron strings? Are there wounds that need to be healed?

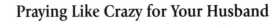

April recognized that Dan's dad had been an emotionally unengaged, uninvolved father who had demanded perfection from his son. There was only one right way to do everything, and Dad expected Dan to always do it the right way. When Dan did things any other way, he heard about it. When he did things right, there was silence. His father never affirmed or encouraged, spoke words of love, hugged, or showed his son that he believed in him and accepted him.

April knew that Dan loved her and their daughters, but realized that because he had never experienced anything but criticism and anger from his own father, he didn't know how to show love and acceptance for his own family. He was demanding, prone to lecture, and always expected the worst from his girls, who were good kids trying to win Daddy's approval—longing for Dad's approval, just as Dan had longed for his father's, a longing he had given up on.

While April had long prayed for Dan's relationship with his daughters to change, she realized that she also needed to pray for Dan's relationship with his dad. She began asking God to heal Dan and help him find his love and acceptance in God as his Father. Eventually, she realized that she also needed to pray for Dan's dad, Fred. "As I was praying for Dan and his relationship with his dad, I suddenly was struck by the thought, *Has Fred ever had anyone who showed him love and acceptance?*" she shares. "I began to pray for Fred, asking God to help him discover how very much God loved him and that he, too, would find healing."

When wounds have been carried on for generations, healing may take time, but we can pray for healing. There are times when our husband may need help in healing the wounds. We can ask God to give him the willingness to seek help. He may not be willing to admit that he is wounded or needs healing. So we begin praying there—asking God to reveal his wounds and needs to him and then give him the desire for healing.

God longs to heal us. He wants us whole. "Long before he laid down earth's foundations, he had us in mind, had settled on us as the focus of his love, to be made whole and holy by his love" (Ephesians 1:4, *The Message*). God longs to make our husbands—and his family and our family—whole. Healed. He not only longs to heal us, but

He wants to redeem the wounds, using them for His glory in our husband's life and in the lives of others as well. We can join Him in this by praying for it, asking God to bring healing to our husbands, our children, us, and all the extended family involved.

Things change

I recently saw an episode of a television sitcom called *The Middle.* I assume "the middle" refers to the main characters being a middle-aged couple with both children to care for and older relatives who also need to be cared for. In this specific episode, the mom is ecstatic that her children are learning to be independent because it may give her a few minutes to recharge herself and not have to be constantly taking care of someone else. Then the phone rings. The children may be becoming more independent, but the older relatives (in this case two aunts) are becoming more dependent.

Life changes. Somewhere along the journey, our parents age. With this aging, grown children may begin to find themselves needing to take care of those who took care of them. They may need to do more things for them. And eventually may need to make decisions about where they should live and the level of care they need. This brings challenges. Not only the physical challenges of now having two homes and two families to take care of, but emotional challenges of seeing parents age. Sometimes the emotional challenges are harder to deal with than the physical. Especially if parents battle diseases and illnesses that take away their physical or mental capacities. It's hard for a child to watch their parent no longer able to take care of themselves—hard to admit and accept.

As our husbands deal with the changing roles and begin taking more responsibility for their parents, we can pray for them—that God will give them the wisdom and patience that they need. We may need to pray for ourselves too. We may need patience as well. And understanding.

Our husbands may struggle with their parents and the growing physical and mental challenges. "I was surprised at how angry Jon would get when he'd visit his mom in the nursing home," Sharon recalls. "She had Alzheimer's, so her thinking was often distorted. She didn't remember who people were or things that had happened. She often seemed to be living in the past. All a part of the disease. But Jon would get mad at her for not remembering and would argue with her. Sometimes it seemed that he thought she was doing it on purpose. He knew she wasn't, but—he just really struggled with it."

Sharon prayed that God would help Jon accept and understand his mom's disease and have wisdom and patience with her. Jon loved his mom and wanted to treat her with honor and respect. His own battle with seeing his mom lose her memory and fade before him was difficult, and like many men, he responded with anger. While the anger seemed to be directed toward his mom, Sharon knew it was really anger at the disease and at the helplessness Jon felt.

God will show us how to pray

Just in our husband's role as a son, there is so much to pray for. The current relationship, if parents are still alive. Healing for any wounds and hurts. The changing roles. The needs of parents as they age. The battle to accept the limitations age and disease place on our parents. The grace to love them well. The need to show honor and respect throughout it all. The busyness that threatens the relationship, as well as all relationships. The grief of losing them.

As we pray for our husband's relationship with his parents, we can ask, "God, how should I be praying for my husband and his parents today? What are the greatest needs?"

Praying Like Crazy for Your Husband

God will answer. He will give us wisdom to know how and what to pray for, and He will move on behalf of our prayers.

Pray for:

- his relationship with his parent(s);
- healing, if needed;
- the specific challenges he faces;
- the changing roles;
- wisdom as he makes decisions about his parents' care;
- patience as he deals with the challenges.

Journal

- What is a favorite memory you have of your own parents while you were growing up?
- Ask your husband to share a favorite memory about his parents while he was growing up.
- Make a list of the specific challenges you see your husband faces in his relationship with his parents. Pray for those challenges.

Guys and Their Friends

Tim and I began dating two years after he graduated from high school. I was impressed that he was still hanging out with friends from his boarding school. Most of my friends had married or gone away to school. I hadn't seen them since graduation. It took a bit of effort for Tim and his friends to get together since they lived some distance away, but they were still doing things together. Motorcycle rides. Fishing trips. Guy things.

Two years later, these friends stood with him at the front of the church. Despite marriages and the birth of children, they continued to get together from time to time. Waterskiing. Camping as families. They helped us build a second story on our home.

They are men who have shared some of the most important years of their lives—from high school through rearing young families. As often happens, life gets busy, and the guys don't talk as often as they once did.

Friends are important. Studies have found that they make us healthier. Not only do they lengthen our lives, but they make that life more enjoyable. They provide support. Courage. A shoulder in tough times. Laughter in good times. Yet studies also reveal that men have fewer of these types of friendships than women have. And as men grow older, the number of friendships they have decreases instead of grows, as it does with women. As women age, they recognize the need for and benefit of friendships and make the time to build strong relationships. Men over thirty tend to lose track of their friends and look to their wives to fill that friendship need.

Male and female friendships are different. My sons noticed this on the elementary school playground. I remember Josh coming home and commenting that the girls broke into little groups—talking, giggling, sometimes excluding others and being mean, while the boys all joined together to play capture the flag or kickball. Talking and connecting is more important than the activity itself for girls, but for guys, the activity is often the connection. They get together to play basketball, hike a mountain, ride bikes, or work on a project. Talking is often centered on the activity, as well. While women may feel they belong as a result of connecting on an emotional level, guys get that sense by being a part of the team.

Even if guys' friendships look different to us and we don't totally get it, friendships are important to men, needed by men, and something we as wives can be praying for.

He and his buddies

If our husbands have friends, we can begin by praying for those friendships, asking God to bless them, grow them, help them to have a positive impact on our guys. We can also pray for our husbands to have a positive impact on their friends.

We can also pray for the friends specifically. We may hear bits and pieces—or whole stories—about their lives and pick up things to pray about. Struggles and battles they may be facing. Physical or spiritual challenges they may wrestle with.

There may be friends who concern us a bit—the language they use, the activities they enjoy, the way they treat women. Sometimes we can't quite pin down the reason why we fear that these friends could negatively influence our husbands. These are things we can pray about instead of worrying about the relationship or reviewing their faults when they come to mind. Just go over them with God and give them to Him. Instead of complaining to our husbands about their friends, talk to God and ask Him to handle it. He may choose to convict our husbands to end the friendship or to confront the friend. He may choose to change the friend—and could possibly use our husbands to set the change in motion. God will do amazing things as we trust Him.

"I wish he had a friend"

Many women have told me that they wish their husbands had friends. But outside of work and talking to the husbands of their wife's girlfriends at get-togethers, many men no longer spend time with the guys. They no longer play sports or do the activities that offer the opportunity for men to hang out. And most men don't call another guy just to talk. Many don't call their wives just to talk.

Wives often resort to "helping" their husbands make friends. Inviting their girlfriends and husbands over hoping the guys will connect. While they may talk well together all evening, most of the time that's the only time men will get together. They're not going to say, "Let's meet for lunch next week." They are not women. Their relationships are typically not driven by connecting emotionally but are more activity or project driven.

So wives attempt to "nudge" their husbands to do things with other guys. "Why don't you call Steve and see if he wants to go kayaking this weekend?" I've tried that kind of "helping." I'm not sure how it's working for others, but it has little results for me. Tim just smiles. Yet I can trust God to bring Tim the friends and opportunities to hang out with other guys.

He brought Steve and his two sons into Tim's life when our sons were at a great age to enjoy biking, hiking, and camping with other guys. The six of them were quite the group. God has brought different friends into Tim's life who have shared his passion for music, even a few who don't live close by, but keep in contact via e-mail and Facebook to talk about Southern Gospel music. As I pray, I trust that God knows the best friends and types of friendships Tim needs. While the results may not look quite like what I think is best, I choose to trust God because I know that He loves my husband even more than I do and knows better than I what Tim needs.

When the job is over

Marie was concerned about Bob. "He just seems so lost since he retired," she shared. "It's like he doesn't know what to do or who he is without work." Marie's concerns aren't unusual. Because men tend to define themselves by what they do—their work—they may lose a sense of who they are and what they're about when they retire. Unlike women, guys often don't have a network of friends to connect with and help them with that sense of who they are. Girlfriends help give a sense of self-esteem and confidence. They remind each other of their value and beauty and offer an I-believe-in-you strength. Because guys don't have friendships like this, they may not have the support system that helps them through transitions such as retirement or job loss or health problems. They tend to turn to their wives for support in these areas.

We can not only ask God to help us be the support they need during these times, but pray for friendships for them. Because retirement allows more time for them to do things they enjoy, it's also a great opportunity for them to meet other men who enjoy doing the same things and to build relationships that can add strength and fun to their lives. Golfing, fishing, traveling—are all things guys can do together. They may meet other men as they volunteer in their communities. We can pray and ask God to open up opportunities and bring the right men who will be fun and a source of strength to our husbands.

More than just buddies

One of my favorite stories of friendship in the Bible is

the story of Jonathan and David. Jonathan must have been a remarkable man who trusted God. He didn't feel threatened by this young man who became an instant hit with the people after killing the giant. Jonathan himself had believed God would defeat enemies in amazing ways and had gone up against the enemy with just his armor bearer. God defeated the Philistines as a result of this trust. But Jonathan didn't get quite the fanfare that David had (1 Samuel 14).

Although Jonathan was next in line to be king, he not only believed that David would be the next king, but he shared that belief with David and willingly committed to serving with him. Jonathan was a friend who wanted what God wanted for David—no matter what it cost him. I believe that was because he had confidence in God to take care of him. He didn't feel the need to worry or strive and push—he just trusted God.

And when David ran for his life, fleeing to the wilderness as Saul hunted him day and night to kill him, "Jonathan, Saul's son, arose and went to David in the woods and strengthened his hand in God" (1 Samuel 23:16, NKJV). He encouraged David, told him not to fear, and helped David hold on to God a little tighter and more confidently.

I pray and ask God to bring Tim friends like Jonathan. Friends who are more than just a buddy to hike with, but someone who will strengthen his grip on God. A godly friend who is connected to God and will encourage Tim in his own journey.

I also pray that God will make Tim a Jonathan for others. That God will help Tim to be a godly friend who gives courage to his friends and supports them in ways that help them to be the men God created them to be. I pray that Tim will be instrumental in helping his friends hold on tighter to God, especially when life is hard.

The obstacles

The devil knows what would happen if godly men got together, encouraged one another, strengthened one another's grip on God, and made life more fun for one another. He doesn't want to see that happen. So he blocks it every way he can.

Busyness is one of the biggest obstacles. Our lives are full. We work more hours than ever before. Our children are involved in more activities than any previous generation—which means parents spend more time carpooling, cheering at sporting events, and supporting other activities. Add to that technology we enjoy—the Internet, e-mail, social networking, etc.—that consumes what little down time we have. Building relationships and getting together with others is pushed out of our lives. We say we want to ("Let's get together soon"), but we fail to make it a priority by actually making the time for it.

We cannot only give our husbands "permission" to take time to do things with friends by encouraging them to do it, but we can pray that God will help them to have the time and opportunities. God can open up calendars or provide opportunities in the busyness. "I had been praying God would bring Ted a friend to talk to and do whatever guys do," Stacey says. "I didn't know how Ted would even have the time to get together with anyone—with working and attending our son's football games. But then he met Bob at one of the games. Bob's son played on the same team. They started talking football and hanging out at practice. Gradually they learned they had a lot in common. They take the boys out for pizza after a game, and all of them hang out together. It's been cool to watch God in action when I wondered how in the world He'd be able to make it happen."

Busyness isn't the only obstacle the devil throws our way. Many times we refuse to risk reaching out to others because of past experiences and lies we believe about ourselves or about how others will respond to us. Our husband may have been rejected by classmates or betrayed by a friend. His insecurities may cause him to feel like no one would really want to be his friend. Or he may believe he has nothing to offer. If he's not into sports, he may struggle with finding common ground with other men. He may not see male friendships as important.

No matter what the obstacle, God can work. He can bring friends who will be Jonathans to them. Or friends to play basketball with or to hike with. He may enable connections with other fathers who are raising sons involved in sports. Sometimes God will bring friends that He desires our husbands to mentor and encourage.

God knows their need. He knows the answers. And He will move on behalf of our prayers, bringing our husbands the friendships that God knows are best for them. As girls, we know the blessing and strength our girlfriends bring us. We can pray that God will give our husbands friends who will strengthen and bless their lives too.

Pray for:

- their friendships and friends;
- the influence of their friends;
- their influence on their friends;
- God to bring them friends;
- godly friendships;
- time to spend with friends;
- God to remove any obstacles.

Journal

- Who are your closest friends? How much time and energy do you put into friendships? What prevents you from spending time with friends?

- Who are your husband's closest friends? How much time and energy does he put into friendships? What prevents him from spending time with friends?

Gifts and Talents, Hopes and Dreams

My husband can sing. He has a beautiful voice and a passion for music. Southern Gospel music. I think he even looks like a Southern Gospel singer. He's been mistaken for one of the musicians when we've been at concerts—people coming up and thanking him for the music that evening, even though he was nowhere near the stage. He has sung at churches, performed for small concerts, and even sang at a women's retreat in Australia. People have affirmed his gift and the blessing it is to them.

It's a gift he didn't really know he had.

After hearing him sing at a church, the music teacher from his high school approached him and wanted to know why he had never joined the choir at school. He laughed. Back in high school he would never have thought about singing in the choir, not only because he was a teenage boy who enjoyed hanging out more than being involved at school, but because he didn't realize the gift God had given him.

A gift we give

I believe that one of the best gifts we can give to others, especially our husbands, is to recognize their gifts and abilities, affirm them, and believe in the possibilities God has for them as they step forward in faith and use those talents. It's hard to believe in ourselves, but when someone else believes in us, we begin to wonder and dream and consider the possibilities. When we believe in our husbands and talk that belief to them, it makes them begin considering the possibilities, the "what ifs," and can give them the courage to take that first step toward what God has for them.

Praying Like Crazy for Your Husband

I'm not sure Tim really believed me when I first began telling him that he had a gift for music. Not only did I tell him he could sing well and that I believed God could use that gift, but I also talked to God about it, asking Him to help Tim recognize the gift himself. I also asked God to give Tim the desire to use the gift. And the courage to give it a try. New things can be scary, especially when you're not sure if you have the ability.

Then I took it a step further and bought Tim a month's worth of voice lessons. I wanted him to have the opportunity to learn the skills that would make him more confident with his ability, and I believed that a teacher would also affirm his gift. His teacher loved him. He'd walk in the door at the end of a long day, and she'd ask, "Please, just sing for me." She taught him skills and breathing techniques and affirmed his gift. He worked with her for several years before she retired. He also attended music schools in Nashville designed specifically for people who want to sing Southern Gospel music. There, he not only learned how to sing better and gained more affirmation that he really had a great voice, but he also met others who shared his passion and understood his love for God, music, and singing. Tim regularly "talks" to these new friends through e-mail and Facebook.

Believing in someone and the possibilities God has for that person is powerful. God has blessed my life with several people who have seen potential in me that I hadn't seen. Their belief and dreams for me became catalysts that gave me the courage to try writing, speaking, and even the job I currently have—a job I had no experience or training for when I was hired. But the person who hired me believed that I could learn and do the job well. If he hadn't believed in me and spoken that belief to me, I might not have ever believed in myself enough to try. He truly *encouraged* me—giving me courage to step out and see what God had for me. It changed my life and opened amazing opportunities. I want to give similar encouragement to others. Especially to my husband.

What are your husband's gifts? What is he a natural at? What causes him to light up and get excited when talks about it or does it? Just the other day my friend Lilly noticed that when I talked about a certain project I was working on, I got more animated and excited. It was a project that brought my passions and my talents together. I love being a part of it! It gives me energy and joy. What gives your husband that? What gets him excited about getting up in the morning and getting to work on it?

It may be a job, but more often, it will be a hobby or ministry that isn't a part of his day job. He may need your prayers for time to be a part of it, belief that it makes a difference, and courage to do it despite the obstacles. It might be possible that God could help it become his job. Matt enjoyed creating video. "I wish I could turn this into a business," he often told his wife, Celia. But he had a job. How could he quit a secure job to risk something he enjoyed doing and was good at? "When they laid me off, I thought, *Well, this is the opportunity that I was hoping for.* Then, I wondered, *Can I do this?"* He signed up for video and editing classes. Celia began praying. "This has to be a God-thing," she reasoned. "So I began praying that God would give me peace and give Matt everything he needed to make a go of this opportunity."

More than just talk

Dreaming God's dreams for others is more than just talking to them and encouraging them that it's possible. Prayer and speaking belief is the first step. The next one can be harder. Putting actions to those words. Supporting their efforts by giving them time to work on their gifts and dreams. It means not resenting the time or energy they need to put into something, especially at the beginning. If he needs classes or tools to help him learn or put his gifts to use, these will require not only time but finances. Are we willing to make sacrifices, both big and small, in order to allow our husbands to pursue God's dreams for them?

There may be times we struggle with it. We'd rather they were at home. We don't want to spend the money. We're not willing to change our lifestyle to make it happen. We may resent the extra burden pursuing his dream puts on us.

Emily went back to work full time so that her husband could go to school full time and pursue his teaching degree. "Chris will make a great teacher," she says. "He has such a passion for kids and just has this knack for helping them to understand. He can take a lesson and create a way to teach it that draws in all the different learning styles. His enthusiasm is contagious." Her smile fades a bit. "I know this is what God wants for him. And I'm excited about it. But there are days when I struggle with working full time, being responsible for all the household chores, and having to run the kids everywhere. He's in an accelerated degree program, so it's very demanding. He tries to help, but between classes and studying—it's just hard. I want this for him, but sometimes I don't want the burden of helping him make it happen."

Emily takes these struggles to God and asks Him to help her have the strength to do what she needs to do. She asks God to help her support Chris and not resent the extra work. She's learned to ask Chris for help around the house—and to let some things go, knowing this is just temporary, even if "temporary" is a couple of years. She believes that God will bless them both. "When Chris comes home from student teaching and shares about his day, he gets so excited about a kid getting something and succeeding. I know God is going to use him powerfully, and that this struggle will be worth the effort." Emily smiles. "He tells me that he is so lucky to have a wife who believes in him and supports him. It's cool to be able to give that to him."

Jonathan gave that to David. Samuel had anointed David king. But Saul was still king. David was just a shepherd boy who played music for King Saul. Jonathan saw God's plan for David; he was drawn to David and believed in him. He showed that belief by giving David his robe, his armor, his sword, bow, and belt. Through these gifts, he was symbolically giving David his own role as prince and recognizing him as next in line to be king (1 Samuel 18).

When David was discouraged or lost sight of God's plan for him, Jonathan was there with words of courage, reminding David of God's plan for him and committing to walk with him all the way.

As wives, we have the opportunity to walk with our husbands on the journey God has for them. Part of our role is to help them become the men God has created them to be. Not by pushing or nagging or telling them how to do it, but by believing in them, seeing the possibilities with them, supporting them as they work toward it, and intentionally and persistently encouraging them.

God will enable us to see the possibilities and will show us how to encourage and support them as we pray. He will give our husbands courage and belief in response to our prayers, as well.

Pray for:

- God to reveal the gifts He's given your husband;
- courage to use the gifts and talents he's been given;
- the opportunity to use them;
- God to show your husband the dreams He dreams for him;
- God to show you how to affirm and support your husband.

Journal

- Make a list of the gifts and talents you see in your husband. How do you see God giving him opportunities to use those abilities?
- Who in your life has given you the gift of believing in you and God's dreams for you? What difference has that made in your life?
- Who else has given this gift to your husband?

The Things That Hinder

It's the craziest thing. I can be upstairs getting ready for work, humming a song, when Tim walks in the room singing the very same song. How does that happen? We didn't listen to the song together. We didn't hear each other humming or singing. But we both have the same song going through our heads.

It amazes me when Tim starts a conversation about something I was just thinking about. Or brings up something from the past that has nothing to do with the moment, yet I was actually just thinking about the same event. Friends once accused us of cheating when playing Pictionary because he drew a line on the paper, and I guessed the answer right away—and it was in no way depicted by just a line.

It happens with couples. We become so connected to each other that we can complete each other's sentences or know what the other one is thinking or feeling. I can tell how Tim is responding in a situation regardless of what is showing on the outside. We know each other.

Most of the time that's fine with me—it reminds me how well we know each other. But other times it's frustrating. Especially when he knows that I'm responding in a negative way and calls me on it. I hate that. Even when I know it's God saying through Tim, *Tami, this is something you need to work on.*

Spouses know each other well. We know things about each other that no one else knows. Good things, like how Tim has this heart for young people and looks for opportunities to connect with them and encourage them. He loves to get teens at our church involved in the sound system and media on Sabbath morning. Spouses know each other's favorite things.

Tim likes berry teas. Chips and salsa are his favorite snack. He loves to hike. The Cathedrals are his all-time favorite singing group.

We wives also know our husbands' weak spots. Their bad habits. The areas they struggle the most. Their woundedness. The temptations they're most prone to battle. The relationships they have that are difficult or painful. Wives know the things that hinder their husbands, keep them from being the men God created them to be.

God longs for us to take this intimate knowledge and pray like crazy for our husbands, asking Him to convict them, heal them, and give them the victories. Paul encourages us to "throw off everything that hinders and the sin that so easily entangles, and let us run with perseverance the race marked out for us" (Hebrews 12:1, NIV). We can turn this verse into a prayer, asking God to help our husbands throw off everything that hinders them and the sin that entangles them, enabling them to run with perseverance, never giving up, always moving forward, even after failures, as they continue to grow and become the men God has created them to be.

Nagging God, not him

Tim used to have a habit that drove me crazy. It sounds like a silly thing, but it annoyed me. He had a tendency to leave cupboard and closet doors open. I know, something pretty small to be complaining about. Especially because the times I noticed it most were on Sunday mornings when Josh was just a toddler and the two of them would fix breakfast. Come on, they were fixing breakfast and I was getting to relax and I'm complaining about open cupboard doors?

But I'm one of those people that has to have everything looking visually just so. Anything out of place disrupts the harmony of the picture and annoys me. I've been known to straighten pictures in the doctor's office because they weren't straight. (This need for a picture-perfect house sometimes annoys Tim.)

So the open doors bugged me.

I had a choice. I could complain to Tim. Get on him to close the cabinets when he had gotten out what he needed in them. I could let it bug me and make me irritated with Tim (and not enjoy the Sunday breakfast as much).

Or I could complain to God.

OK, so I actually did talk to God about open cabinet doors. It sounds silly, but there's a lesson here I need to point out. Sometimes our husband's habits are merely annoying. They don't hurt anything in the scheme of things. A friend of mine would've given anything to have a husband who could leave cupboard doors open after cancer made her a widow way too young.

We can take these annoying habits to God. Ask Him to change our husbands or to change us. Help him to close the door or to give me peace about it. Somewhere along the way, Tim has learned to close the cupboard doors. I'm not even sure when it happened, but for a while, I practiced closing the doors and saying, "Thank You, Lord, for a husband who made breakfast this morning."

We can nag God—or we can nag our husbands. Often nagging our husbands will irritate them, making two people frustrated. And sometimes nagging causes the other person to just dig in and refuse to do anything about it. Nagging God gets better results all the way around.

Speaking up

There are times, however, when we need to speak up. Our husband is doing something that's more than an annoying habit. He's hurting himself or someone else.

Amber's husband, Dan, battles anger. When one of their daughters does something wrong, Dan yells at her.

More than once the scene has left a little girl crying and Dan defensive. "He doesn't realize how afraid the girls are of him," Amber worries.

Caleb never thought it would turn into a problem. A drink with the guys after work once in a while. But once in a while turned into every night. Kristie sees changes in Caleb and is concerned that he doesn't even realize what's happening.

Diana doesn't know what possessed her to check the history on Dave's computer. He was spending more and more time in his office and less and less time engaging with the family. When he was with her, he acted irritated and frustrated with her. One click and she uncovered what had her husband's attention. "I couldn't believe that he was looking at porn," she cries. "I didn't know what to do. I got on my knees and began praying. Then I confronted him."

There are times when a wife needs to confront her husband. It's part of loving well.

Some of us avoid confronting at all costs. We turn a blind eye, tell ourselves it really isn't that bad, or try to go behind him and fix what we can instead of dealing with it. This enables the sin and its influence to continue. Allowing behavior that hurts him or others is not loving well. We are called to be our husbands' helpers, not their enablers. Sometimes love speaks up.

How we speak up can make all the difference. Our words and tone of voice will convey much. It's important that we speak from love and not from anger. We need God's help. We must pray and ask God to give us wisdom to know what to say, when to say it, and then ask Him to be with us and do the talking through us. There are times when the problem is so serious and big that we may want another person with us. Again, as we talk to God, He will give us wisdom in knowing whom to ask and then will guide us as we confront our husbands in love. It is more loving to confront them about sin in a caring, intentional way, than it is to allow them to continue sinning because we don't want to make them mad.

Even in trials show honor

As women, we love to talk. And we often tell our girlfriends everything that's happening in our lives, including things about our relationship with our husbands and the way he makes us mad and the things he does that concern us. We need to be careful in this area. It is sometimes helpful to talk to someone. Sometimes we need that "reality" check to know for sure that we're not crazy and that yes, this is something to be concerned about. I sometimes call my friend Linda and say, "OK, I need a reality check here . . ." One of the great things about friends is the strength and courage they bring to our lives.

However, we need to be careful with whom we talk about our husbands. They must be people we trust who will not share what we say with others, won't judge our husbands and treat them differently, but who will support us and pray with us for our husbands and the situation. Truly caring and loving both of us. The safest person to talk with about our husbands is God. He will never stop loving them or us and will work in powerful ways in each of our lives.

God has commanded us to honor our husbands. This command isn't based on their behavior. So even during times of trials or even when they're failing us or struggling with sin, we want to show them honor by the way we talk about them and by respecting them enough to not make them a topic of gossip. If you need someone to talk to, ask God to give you godly women whom you can trust who will pray with you and pray for your husband, caring and believing God will work in his life.

A time to fast

There are some things that hold on to us tightly and won't let us go. Addictions. Sin. The impact of past wounds. Even after praying and praying, nothing seems to really change. We don't understand and don't know what to do.

The disciples faced this same dilemma. A father brings his demon-possessed son to them for healing, and they can't heal him. Nothing happens. They do what they've done in the past, but the boy still falls on the ground and convulses. Why? Why didn't God heal him? It's something God would want for the boy.

They ask Jesus, "Why couldn't we cast out the demon? Why didn't it work for us?"

He responds, "This kind can come out by nothing but prayer and fasting" (Mark 9:29, NKJV).

At times we need to do more than just pray, but truly commit to prayer through fasting. If it was true for Jesus and the disciples, it is true for us. There may be moments when we need to be in prayer and fasting for our husbands as they battle the things that hinder them.

As I shared in my book *Praying Like Crazy for Your Kids*, fasting has been a discipline I have always practiced—but didn't always understand. In the beginning of my journey with prayer and fasting, I thought it just meant getting through the day without food. But it is so much more than that!

First, fasting does not have to be from food or completely from food. You may choose to fast from food for a day or part of a day or may decide to fast from certain foods that you really enjoy, such as chocolate, sugar, snacking in between meals, a favorite beverage, etc. But fasting doesn't have to be about food. We can also fast from habits, television, Internet, social networking, reading certain materials, radio—anything that is a part of our day. I have fasted from food, but more often than not because I tend to fast for an extended period of time, I typically choose to fast from something in particular. Some choices have included chocolate, caffeine, listening to the radio on the way to work, reading anything but the Bible, and snacking in between meals.

But choosing how to fast is only part of the equation. The second part is more important.

Fasting means replacing whatever you've chosen to fast from with prayer. Saying No to something that you enjoy or indulge in regularly and taking the time you would've spent eating, reading, or watching that favorite television program and instead, praying. Too often I've just skipped whatever and used that time to do something else. That's not a spiritual fast.

How long do you fast and pray?

That's a decision between you and God. Sometimes I have chosen to fast until I believe God has answered. Or until the fast becomes a habit—I'm no longer turning the radio off and praying; instead, I'm just not listening to the radio. Or I'm not even thinking about that midafternoon snack. Once skipping something becomes a habit, I choose to end the fast or switch to something else. Because again, it's not about what I'm doing without, but that I'm praying instead. Skipping something becomes a trigger to pray. When the trigger doesn't work, it's time to stop or change triggers.

There are times that I choose to fast and commit to a certain period of time—it could be a day, a week, a month, or forty days (popular because of Jesus' forty days of fasting and prayer). I tend to pray about it first, asking God how long I should fast. I commit the fast to God. I never want it to be about me, about *my* fasting and prayer being what makes the difference. It has to be about God. He alone can make the difference. My commitment to fasting and prayer is about God and me. It's not a magical formula so I can get what I want. It's more about drawing close to God, being committed about something, and seeking His will and His answers.

Not all fasting ends the way I'd like. Sometimes my prayers appear to go unanswered. Nothing changes. But I know that something does change. It changes in me. As I fast and pray, I am wrestling with God in a way, seeking His will, learning to trust Him more completely, giving up my own desires and wishes and trusting Him to do what's eternally best.

As wives fast for their husbands, I believe it deepens not only our commitment to God and trust in Him, but it strengthens our commitment to our husbands as well and deepens our love for them. It's hard to not care about someone you're praying for, but when you already love them and are praying for them, it just takes it deeper.

Power in prayer

Prayer does change things. God tells us that we don't have because we don't ask. He promises that if we ask, He will give. And because God desires our husbands to be "whole and holy" (Ephesians 1:4, *The Message*), our prayers and fasting for those things that hinder them, that slow them down, that get in the way of God's plan and will for them, are prayers He longs to answer. Will answer. Does answer.

As we look to Jesus, He will enable our husbands to run the race with strength and courage and victory.

He has given us the opportunity to pray for victory for our husbands like no one else can. We know them better than anyone else does. We know their struggles and their wounds. It is our privilege to fight for them. We are a team. Husbands and wives. Heading toward a finish line together. Fighting for each other, asking God to get rid of all the obstacles in our paths and our hearts. It may be one of the biggest responsibilities we have in marriage. A responsibility and opportunity to stand beside our husbands and fight for them in prayer.

Pray for:

- those bad habits, sinful tendencies, etc., that your husband deals with;
- God to show you how to be a support and help;
- the wisdom to know what to say, when to say it, what to do and how;
- strength to say No to the temptations he faces—pornography, alcohol, workaholism, etc.;
- forgiveness for your husband;
- healing from the affect of sin and from its wounds.

Journal

- What victories have you seen God give your husband in his battle with sin?
- Make a list of the little bad habits that annoy you. Pray over them and give them to God.
- Is there an area in which your husband struggles and can't seem to gain the victory? Commit to a time of prayer and fasting. Journal what God teaches you during this time.

Relationship With God

Tim recently shared his testimony at church. Our pastor had asked him to preach. He prayed about it. No sermon idea came. But he felt impressed to just share what God had done in his life.

It was powerful. Testimonies of how God has worked in a life usually are. He told how he had grown up in the church. Knew all the rules. And that was pretty much what he lived. The rules. It was all about obedience. And in the areas where he didn't obey, he felt guilt. He told the congregation that while the outside looked good, he realized he was pretty unhappy inside.

Then came a turning point in his life. What looked like a small tragedy turned out to be a huge blessing.

February 16, 1990. Tim was working on cable lines. Cutting wires that ran to homes. His company was changing out lines. His bucket truck was in the shop that day, so he was hooking his ladder on the main line and cutting the wires that ran to the houses. When he cut the last line, the tension in the main line changed; it was no longer being pulled toward the houses. His ladder moved forward with the line and Tim fell backward, two stories, onto the sidewalk below. A man in one of the houses saw it happen. One moment Tim was on the ladder; the next he was on the ground.

Tim had put his hands out to cushion his landing. The bones of his wrists, which had taken the brunt of the fall, were crushed. He knew by looking at them it was bad. His first words to me when I arrived in the emergency room were, "They're going to cut off my hands." (They didn't.)

Tim shared with the congregation the fears he had faced in the emergency room. The worry of how he'd support his young family—our sons were four and one at the time, and I was a stay-at-home mom. The fear of not having the use of his hands again. The possibility of not being able even to take care of himself.

Then came the moment. The turning point.

In the middle of the night, lying totally helpless in a hospital bed, his arms in slings tied to bars on the side of his bed causing him to look like he was reaching to the ceiling, Tim realized that he hadn't been reaching up to God. He'd been doing it all himself, relying on his strength and his ability to keep the rules. And it was only making him miserable. Now here he lay, totally dependent on others to do everything for him. He realized his need for total dependence on God and was overwhelmed by the love and grace he felt wash over him.

His life changed in that moment as he gave himself completely to God that night. He stopped trying to keep the rules and started allowing God to work in him. Started recognizing God's love and grace and how it could change his life.

Before the fall

As I listened to Tim share his story, I was reminded of the part of the story that wasn't being said. What happened before the fall. What came before that powerful night.

As a young wife, I was watching my husband work and work and work—and saw how miserable he was. Felt it. He was working two jobs at the time. Working on cable lines all day and then trying to start his own business at night.

He was busy. Too busy for things that were really important. Like God. I watched as he spent less and less time with God. I didn't think he even realized it was happening.

So I began praying. Asking God to do whatever it took

to make him realize where he was headed and where he needed to be. My friend Janet joined me. We began praying together in January, begging God to help Tim recognize his need for a deeper, more intimate relationship with God.

A month and half later, God answered dramatically.

Not everyone falls

God does not answer everyone's prayers so dramatically, but He does answer everyone's prayers. Not everyone needs dramatic answers. Some husbands are walking closely with God. Others may talk the talk, but not walk the walk. And still others may not be interested in God at all. As wives, we have the opportunity to pray for our husbands and their relationships with God no matter where they are—and we may know better how to pray specifically for their walk.

How is your husband's relationship with God? Does he spend time with God daily? Occasionally? Are there areas of his spiritual walk that he struggles with? What does he believe about God? What keeps him from walking more closely with God?

Pray specifically

Knowing the answers to these questions can help guide you as you pray for your husband. It's one of the benefits of being a wife—having better knowledge of how to pray and what to pray for.

What keeps him from walking more closely with God? Busyness? Disinterest? Not really knowing how to spend time with God?

Pray specifically for those things.

Begin by praying that God will give your husband the

desire to spend time with Him. The desire to grow closer to God is the first step. He may *know* that he *should,* but he may still not really *want* to. Ask God to soften your husband's heart, give him a hunger for more of God, for something deeper. Ask the Holy Spirit to reveal His need and give him the *desire* to have it filled and the assurance that God alone can fill it.

If busyness is a problem, pray that God will help provide the time—and that He would give him the desire to make the time. We all have the time for what is truly important to us. We *make* time for those things. Our husbands may make the time for the Sunday night football game, time to surf the Net, play a pickup game of basketball with friends on Thursday night, or play his guitar. We often let time with God go because we feel so busy, and we really don't realize how important it is. We may *say* it's important, but how we live our schedules shows that it's the first thing to go, the first thing we put off when we're running behind or have things to do. Ask God to help your husband make time with Him the priority in his life.

Are there specific things using up his time that could be eliminated? Such as TV or the computer? Instead of nagging your husband, take it to God. Ask God to show your husband how to better use his time in order to make room for the things that really matter—such as time with God. Ask God to convict your husband of time wasters and give him a hunger to know God more, a desire to get into His Word.

Maybe he does walk closely with God and does spend time with God, but has struggles in certain areas. Perhaps prayer or Bible study. Maybe he struggles to really believe and live in the certainty that God loves him. Maybe he is focused on the rules instead of relationship. Or maybe he doesn't have godly men that he can talk to, grow with, pray with. Pray for those areas. Ask God to guide your husband and teach him how to deepen his understanding and walk. Pray that he will experience God's love in new ways and be able to comprehend how deep and wide and high and big God's love is for him. Give God his struggle with the rules and ask that God will give him freedom and show him how to trust God to make him righteous. Invite God to bring godly men into your husband's life who will walk with him, hold him accountable, and encourage his walk.

Ask your husband how you can pray more specifically for his walk with God. Tell him that you're praying for him and his walk with God and ask him if there are any specific needs or struggles.

When your husband doesn't believe

What if your husband doesn't believe in God? Or believes but sees no need for a relationship with Him? "Yeah, that's nice, but it's not for me." How do you pray?

Begin by praying for yourself. Ask God to help you to be a witness to your husband. The Bible tells us that wives can win their husbands over without preaching, nagging, or saying a word, but by their behavior (see 1 Peter 3:1, 2).

We begin by having our own intimate and personal relationship with God. Not just a now-I-lay-me-down-to-sleep praying relationship; not just a I-read-my-Bible-for-half-an-hour relationship, but a dynamic, growing, healing, personal relationship that makes God the center of our lives and causes us to find healing and growth in our lives. A relationship that meets our core needs of love, acceptance, and value. When we are walking closely with God, taking our needs, wounds, struggles, and dreams to Him, He will give us a peace and joy that will permeate our lives in such a way that people, including our husbands, will be drawn to Him. They will want what we have. This type of relationship with God will also free us from looking to our husbands to make us happy all the time—a humanly impossible task.

As God heals and fills you, ask Him to show you how to love your husband the way He does. Ask for eyes to see him the way God does. From our human perspective, we see things differently from the way God does. We hear a person who is always bragging about their latest promotion, great new "toy," etc., and we think they are arrogant. God may instead see a hurting person who is trying desperately to find value and acceptance and thinks if he can impress someone with his accomplishments, then maybe he'll find value. We may do the same thing with our spouses—looking at the outward behavior and not seeing past to the hurt or wounds that are the root of the problem.

As God shows us our husbands through His eyes, we can pray for healing and growth in those things. For instance, asking God to help our husbands find value in God. But seeing him through God's eyes can also help us to love him as God loves him. Ask God to give you unconditional love for your husband. To give you the strength and the desire to love him no matter what, no matter how he's acting, no matter what he's saying. This is impossible to do without God doing it through us.

Then pray like crazy for his salvation.

Pray that God will convict him of his need for God. That God will soften his heart and give him a desire to know Him. Ask God to bring people and experiences into his life that will influence him and draw him to God.

Thank God that He is working, because He is. Even when you can't see anything happening, God is leading and drawing your husband. He will relentlessly pursue your spouse to capture his heart completely. He desires your husband's salvation even more than you do. Trust Him. Believe that He is working and "talk" like it in your thoughts. Reminding yourself that God hears your prayers and is at work will bring you peace. This peace will be a witness to your husband too. Don't nag him to go to church or read His Bible or whatever it is you think he should be doing. Instead, take it to God and trust God to lead and guide your husband to Him.

Spiritual leaders

God intended for husbands to be the spiritual leaders of their homes. Their walk with God is incredibly important—it will influence their wives and children, as well as those around them. If they're not walking closely, they won't be teaching their families to walk closely. We can pray for our husbands to be the spiritual leaders God has designed them to be.

Many times a husband knows that God has made him the leader of the home, but he really doesn't know how to lead spiritually. He may not have seen it done while he was growing up. Sometimes what a wife expects from her husband in the role of spiritual leader isn't what he is convicted to do. She may think a spiritual leader leads worship every night after supper. He may not have a clue how to keep a couple of kids interested in God through worship. If he tries, he may feel like he's failing because he's just reading something that they're not getting or enjoying. And if he feels like a failure, he will most likely quit and not try again.

Ask God to guide your husband to know what his role as spiritual leader should look like. Trust God to answer and lead him. Ask God to help your husband walk closely with Him so that his life example alone leads your family. Then if you're better at engaging the kids in worship, be responsible for family worship. Or take turns as a family being responsible, giving the kids a chance to lead. Being a spiritual leader is more than reading something for family worship. It's a way of life. It requires a man to pray for his family, to lead by his example of walking with God and to make decisions for his family based on how he sees God leading. Pray for these things. That God will show him how to pray for his family. That God will guide him in decision-making.

To allow husbands to be the spiritual leaders God has designed them to be may require us as wives to ask God to convict us of expectations that are ours and not God's. Ask His help in laying aside those expectations. When our sons were little, I thought that being the spiritual leader of our home meant that Tim should lead family worship. Yet he didn't have the ideas to be creative and engage two active boys or the time to find the resources needed. I did. Sometimes I found resources and gave them to him to use. Other times, it worked for me to lead or read a Bible story. We found it fun to let the boys be responsible too. They loved entertaining us with Bible stories they'd act out as charades and have us guess. I needed to learn that Tim didn't have to be responsible for coming up with all the ideas and leading out all the time. I needed to release my husband from that expectation and simply pray that God would guide him as the spiritual leader of our home, trusting that God would give him what he needed to do what God had called him to do.

Pray scripture

As we pray for our husbands, we can turn to God's Word to help us know how to pray for them and their relationship with God.

The apostles gave us examples in prayers they prayed for other believers, asking God to deepen their walk with Him, encouraging them and challenging them. As we read and pray through their letters to believers, we can turn their words into prayers for our husbands.

"Thank You, God, for my husband and the gifts You've given him. Thank You for the ways You use him to enrich our family and our church. Keep him strong to the end (see 1 Corinthian 1:4–9).

"Father, please give my husband spiritual wisdom so that he can grow in his relationship with You. Help him to understand the hope that is found in You. Help him to understand the power that comes from walking with You (see Ephesians 1:17–19).

"Empower him with inner strength through Your Spirit. Help him to trust in You. Let his roots grow down into Your love and keep him strong. And may he have the power to understand, as all God's people should, how wide, how long, how high, and how deep Your love for him is. May he experience the love of Christ, though it is too great to understand fully. Then he will be made complete with all the fullness of life and power that comes from God" (see Ephesians 3:14–19).

As we read and study God's Word, we'll come across other prayers, promises, and scriptures we can use to guide us in praying for our husbands.

"God, give my husband singleness of heart for You. Put a new spirit within him. Give him a tender, responsive heart (see Ezekiel 11:19).

"Father, help him to realize and believe that You have chosen him from before the foundations of the world to be the focus of Your love. Make him whole and holy by Your love as he lives it and believes it each day" (see Ephesians 1:4–6).

We can pray through Galatians 5:22, 23 and ask God to grow the fruit of the spirit in his life and make it evident. Wives can cover their husbands in God's armor as they head into their day by praying through Ephesians 6:10–17, maybe even smiling as they picture their spouse dressed in armor.

Scripture can serve as a guide as we pray for our husbands to walk closely with God and really know Him.

God longs for his heart

God loves to answer prayers for people to know Him, grow deeper in Him, walk with Him, understand His love, and commit completely to Him. Those are His desires for our husbands. He sent His Son, not only to die on the cross to pay the price for our salvation and give us eternal life, but to live a life that revealed more clearly who the Father is, what He's like. God longs for people to really, truly know Him. As we pray for our husbands to walk as intimately and closely with God as a human being can know God, He will answer. As we trust Him to do whatever it takes, including falling and shattering his wrists, God will move on the hearts of our husbands and draw them deeper.

Pray for:

- them to know God in a real and intimate way;
- them to have a desire to spend time with God and grow in their relationship with Him;
- God to clear their schedule so that they have time;
- God to teach them how to spend time with Him;
- godly male friends to walk with them and hold them accountable;
- their salvation if they are not a believer;
- them to be the spiritual leaders God designed them to be.

Journal

- Where is your husband in his walk with God?
- How are you seeing God work in your husband's life spiritually?
- What are the strengths of his relationship with God?
- What are the struggles?
- What are the biggest hindrances in his walking closely with God?

Praying Like Crazy for Your Husband

- What areas of his spiritual walk do you want to pray for more specifically?
- How will you commit to praying for your husband's spiritual walk?

The Problems of Marriage

Some of my favorite marriage books have interesting titles: *Opposites Attack* and *Love and War.* Not very romantic, huh? Doesn't conjure up pictures of happily ever after and romantic dinners by the fire. But most marriages aren't all romance and happily-ever-after. Every marriage has struggles, fights, battles, disagreements, hurts, or "discussions," depending on what a couple chooses to call those moments of conflict.

That was a new thought for my friend Karla. She knew her marriage had its share of struggles and difficulties. As a new Christian, she was excited to learn and grow. So she joined a women's Bible study and prayer group. "Do you all struggle in your marriages too?" she asked one evening. "I thought Christian marriages were perfect, and you wives never got mad at your husbands."

We laughed. The room was filled with godly women who loved their husbands and their children, women who were leaders in various areas at church. But yes, we have all struggled in our marriages. There have been times when we have been mad at our husbands, hurt by them, and maybe even questioned if we wanted to remain married to them.

Despite the battles and tough times, we were also all committed to our marriages and our husbands, praying through those times and praying for God to bring healing and growth and love into those moments.

The real enemy

When we are in the middle of an argument or are experiencing hurt and pain because of something our husbands have said or done, it's easy to forget that we're in a battle and that we have an enemy. At that moment, our husbands feel like the enemy. And we typically and naturally respond to that emotion. We forget that we're both on the same side, that these are the men who love us more than anyone else, and that we love them and are committed to them.

Different personalities handle conflict and hurt in their own ways. We may argue, scream, or fight. Others will attempt to reason and explain and defend—trying to talk out the problem and get him to see our side of the story (and often, to see that he's wrong.) Those who can't stand conflict may deal with it by withdrawing or going silent—ignoring the conflict and the husband. Icy silence speaks louder than words sometimes. And others may just not deal with it, choosing instead to passively go along with their husbands, pushing down the anger and hurt as it slowly builds walls of bitterness.

Regardless of how we choose to handle conflict, our brains are thinking—typically thinking—negative thoughts such as, *He doesn't really love me,* or, *I'd be better off without him.* Or, *I just wish I'd never married him,* or, *Why am I always the one to blame whenever anything happens? Why doesn't he take responsibility?* The list goes on.

The enemy has a field day with conflict in marriages. His intent is to divide and conquer. He wants to destroy our marriages. He will use anything he possibly can to push and manipulate us into conflicts and tempt us to think thoughts that could destroy our marriages. That's his goal.

He knows our weaknesses—not only individually, but as a couple—and uses them for his good. He knows those things that will set us off, those things we find ourselves fighting about the most—whether it's finances, raising the children, where we go on vacation, or a home project, he knows where we think differently and uses it as a wedge. God designed us to be different from each other so that our differences balance each other and help us grow. The devil will use those differences to divide us and destroy us.

Getting us at odds with each other is only the beginning of his plan. He will make sure we feel hurt, not heard, or misunderstood so that we will become defensive, feel sorry for ourselves, bring up past hurts, and doubt the other person's love. He will tempt us to believe that we'd be happier if we weren't married and anything else he can get us to think in order to enlarge the separation the conflict has created.

How many times did one small incident turn into something so much bigger—and we found ourselves angry at each other for hours or days? A fight over something silly, and we retreated into our own areas of the house and didn't speak the rest of the day?

We have an enemy—and it's not our husbands. Sometimes we forget how real the enemy is. We rarely live like we have an enemy out to destroy us and our relationships. The Bible tells us that the enemy is like a roaring lion, seeking to devour; and it cautions us to resist him (see 1 Peter 5:8). We often live like he doesn't exist.

We need to pray, asking God to help us remember that an enemy does exist and does want to destroy us, to be aware of our enemy even in those moments of conflict, and to help us not treat our husbands like the enemy.

When we're in the heat of a conflict, we may not feel like praying. Especially not together. But that is a time when we must be aware of our need to invite God into the moment and ask Him to bind the devil. We must resist giving into the devil's lies and allow him to divide us.

Who's right? Who's wrong?

When we're in the middle of a conflict, we're typically thinking about our side, what we think is right, and how the other person is wrong. It's me versus him. We both want our way. Here again, prayer will help us walk toward healing and reconciliation as we pray and ask

God to convict both of us where we're wrong and where the other person is right. We can ask Him to show us where we're right, as well, especially if we are the type of personality that so dislikes conflict that we typically just give in to the other person regardless, and ask for the wisdom and courage to push for what is right in a loving and kind way.

It may be easier to pray and ask God to convict our husbands where they're wrong, "Lord, show him that he's wrong; help him to see it my way!" But it's important to ask God to convict us as well, to help us see where we need to give, change our minds, and admit our wrong.

We can ask God to help us see, hear, and understand our husband's perspective. I've found it also helps to pray that God will show us common ground. Often we want the same thing; we're just approaching from different ways. Tim and I have sometimes disagreed on how to handle a situation with one of our sons. We're two different personalities, and we parent differently as a result. He thinks I'm too soft; I think he's too hard. It's been very helpful for us to first remember that we both want the same thing—for our son to learn a certain lesson or to be responsible in the current situation. Reminding ourselves that we're on the same side and have the same goal takes some of the tension from the situation and allows us to then more calmly talk about how we need to get there, giving us the opportunity to hear the other person's thoughts and viewpoints as a possibility and not as a threat against what we want.

Healing begins as we learn to step back and look at what the conflict is about, find common ground—things we agree on—and look for a solution that works for both of us. If only one of us "wins," then the marriage hasn't won. We can ask God to help us in this—to help us put aside our self and seek what's best both for our marriage and for the conflict at hand.

It's about us, not me

It's been a tough week for me. I was away for a few days for a video-editing class. By the time I arrived home, I wasn't feeling well. The doctor said I had an infection and prescribed an antibiotic. So for the past couple of days, I've been juggling work, writing, pain from the infection, and now side effects from the antibiotic. Just hasn't been fun.

So in the middle of writing this chapter, I needed to stop, just as I was getting on a roll, and fix lunch for us so that Tim could get to school. I really didn't want to stop. The devil tempted me to think, *Why am I always the one who has to stop my work? Why can't he?* I pushed it aside as best I could (should've prayed about it!) and fixed lunch.

First thing Tim said at the table, "That's a lot of rice."

Did I say it had been a bad week?

I took his words personally. What I heard him say was, "You fixed too much food again." (This has been a topic of discussion before.) Then the devil stepped in and picked up on that thought I hadn't prayed about but had just pushed aside and allowed to lurk in my brain. *Why am I always the one who has to stop what she's doing to fix lunch? Why can't he? He's just studying for class. He knows how hard I'm working to get this project done this week. Why doesn't he offer to help? But no, I'm the one that has to stop and make the meals or whatever. And now he's saying that I don't do that right, I fix too much food.*

Tim could tell right away that I was mad. I'm not always good at hiding it.

"What's wrong? Did that make you mad?"

It had. On another day, I might have been able to pass it off and not let it bother me, not let it make me feel as if I wasn't measuring up to his expectations or that I had failed again. The feeling that I'll never be enough is one of the lies I battle constantly. Or that I'm too much.

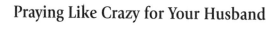

The devil knew. He knew I was not feeling well physically and that I was working hard to complete a project. Maybe he thought it was even funny that he could get us to be mad at each other over something silly while I was in the middle of writing about praying for the conflicts in marriage. Regardless, he knew that one simple comment from Tim—and I was in the perfect frame of mind to take it personally.

Now I should also say it's been a tough week for Tim. His wife had been away for five days. He's preparing for finals at school—his first finals in more than thirty years. Plus he was worried about my health. What if it wasn't just an infection? What if it was worse? There was a possibility that it was something more, and treating it as an infection was just the first step. He loves me and was letting the what-ifs get the best of him. I'm sure he saw my reaction to his comment about the rice and thought, *Now what did I say? I've blown it again, haven't I? Why does she take everything so personally? I can't win.*

I tried to explain that his comment was just piling on top of a lot of other frustrations, but I saw him pull back too. Begin to get mad at the situation. All over a bowl of rice. (And yes, I had made more than what two people could eat because I planned on having the leftovers for my son's dinner when he got home from work. Tim just didn't know what I was thinking.)

It's typical. We forget or don't know where the other person is coming from or what's happening in their lives at that moment, and we take what they say and do personally. Even when it's not meant that way.

We so need God to give us wisdom and insight into understanding our spouses in each situation and need His help in not taking things personally. I often ask God to protect me, to help me not take things personally, but to let them roll off like water rolls off a duck. (I like visuals.) I don't want to let the devil win. I don't want to give him room to cause conflict that can weaken our relationship with each other or cause us to retreat and not support each other when we need it. This week, Tim needs my support as he finishes classes, and I need his as I attempt to get my body healthy again.

Marriage is about "us." It's not about me and my getting everything I want my way. When we're married, we become "one" and our goal, even in conflict or especially in conflict, is to resolve it in a way that's best for both of us. This will require me to set aside self and to not take things personally. Honestly, it's a task only God can accomplish.

We need to forgive

As we work our way through conflicts, we will need to forgive. And we may need to ask our husbands to forgive us. We can ask God to help us forgive our husbands for hurting us, but we may also need to ask for forgiveness—from our spouses and God—for things we've done, words we shouldn't have said, things spoken in anger that hurt our husbands, or for the silence and unwillingness to deal with the conflict that hurt the relationship.

In moments when we don't want to forgive, we can ask God to give us the willingness, praying for the desire to forgive. Prayer always begins where you honestly are. If you don't want to forgive, tell God. Be honest. "Lord, I really don't want to forgive him right now. He's . . ." Talk to God about it. Explain what you are feeling. And ask Him to work in your heart and give you the attitude that He desires.

Forgiveness is a gift we give ourselves. It releases us from bitterness. It gives us freedom from the hold that refusing to forgive has—a hold that brings pain and anger and that allows the situation or person to continue to affect us.

But forgiveness is also a gift we give to our spouses. It

can help release them from guilt. It can remind them that they are loved and be a reminder of God's unconditional love and forgiveness.

Asking for forgiveness when we've done wrong will be harder for some more than for others. Some of us ask for forgiveness for things that aren't really even ours or don't need forgiveness. But some of us have a hard time admitting wrong, taking responsibility, saying "I'm sorry" for the hurts and pain we've caused, and asking for forgiveness. Sometimes we just say "I'm sorry" and that's enough. Other times we may need to actually ask, "Will you forgive me? I know I've caused you pain and I'm sorry."

When we find it hard to ask, again, we can take it to God. *Lord, I know that I've hurt my husband. I know that I need his forgiveness. But it's hard to ask.* Give it to God and ask Him to give you the courage and, if needed, to lay down the pride that stands in the way.

It's not always easy

Not all disagreements in marriage are as simple as a question about rice. There are times when a conflict or betrayal is so huge it will take a miracle for the marriage to survive. There are times when no one would blame you for walking away. There will be times when walking away from a marriage is necessary. Abuse is one of those times. If a husband is abusing his wife, she needs to get help and find a safe place. He may repeatedly say he's going to get help and that he loves her and he's sorry, but until he really does get help and begins to change, she needs to protect herself and any children involved.

There are times when a husband chooses to walk away from a marriage. I've watched this happen in the lives of several of my friends—godly, beautiful women who loved their husbands and never wanted their marriages to end. Several of those men have remarried, yet my friends continue to pray for them, continuing to ask God to bless them, grow them, and draw them close to Him. They inspire me with their courage. I've seen glimpses of the pain their husbands have caused in their lives, yet they continue to pray and care.

As always, we need to pray for wisdom. Wisdom to know when to stay and forgive and work on the marriage, praying like crazy all the way through the dark time. Wisdom to know when to walk away, even temporarily, and seek help.

Anne is praying for wisdom now. She has chosen to stay in her marriage despite finding out about her husband's affair. "Am I crazy for staying?" she asked me recently. Her husband has confessed and asked her forgiveness. He's told her that he wants to work through this and be the man she deserves. He's going to counseling. But it's hard. Learning of her husband's affair has left her with a myriad of feelings—ranging from anger to feeling like she just wasn't enough. She's not sure what it will take to trust him again. She wonders if she ever will completely trust him. Will she be able to believe him when he says he's working late? Or will she fear that he's meeting someone else? Will she always feel insecure and that she's just not enough to hold his attention?

There are no easy answers. For Anne's situation or for many others. Life is hard. Every one of us makes choices that affect people around us, including our spouses. When they choose to have physical or emotional affairs or to walk away from God or become involved in an addiction, such as alcohol, drugs, or pornography, it affects us, our lives, and our feelings toward them.

Even when we want to forgive and move forward, the consequences of people's actions will still be there. Anne's trust will have to be rebuilt slowly and over time. It will be hard. Friends tell her, "Just move on; you have every right." There's a part of her that wants to quit and move on. But another part of her wants to stay and fight. "There are days when I hate him for what he's done to us, but I still love him," she admits.

Staying will be hard. So will leaving. Both will bring their own problems and challenges. Leaving isn't an easy answer.

"I know it's hard, but I believe God will bless you if you stay," I answer Anne.

"How do I get through this?" she asks me in tears.

"Pray like crazy," I tell her. "Lean on God. Tell Him the truth about what you're feeling. Tell Him you are angry and hurt. Tell Him you're angry and hurt at your husband. Tell Him that you're angry at Him for not preventing this. Give it to Him. Tell Him you think you want to leave, but that you also want to stay. Ask Him to give you peace and wisdom and courage. He will take care of you. He will redeem this situation."

Real healing from conflict, whether big or small, comes from laying aside self, seeking what's best for both of you, and offering transparency and willingness.

Transparency in who you are, what you're feeling, and how you are processing what's happening. If you hold things back or aren't honest about what you're feeling, complete resolution might not happen. And every little bit of unresolved conflict will tend to pile up in a corner of your heart. With each conflict, that corner will grow more cluttered with those unresolved hurts and issues until the corner can't contain it, and it explodes into your life. We need to be transparent with our husbands and with God. There may be times when our husbands don't feel like a safe place to us. Perhaps they haven't treated our feelings with respect before; how do we trust them with our feelings now? But we can always trust God with our real hearts, and we can ask Him to make our husbands a safe place and to give us wisdom in being transparent with them.

Then we need willingness. Willingness to do what it takes for resolution and healing. Sometimes only God can give us that willingness. But He will give it to us as we pray and ask.

Love and war

So far, my favorite book on marriage has been John and Stasi Eldridge's *Love and War.* It doesn't sound like a title of a book on marriage, but it is. They go past the "make a regular date night" and "say 'I feel' not 'you always' " and get to the real heart of what impacts marriages. We have an enemy. He has wounded us, and we've brought those wounds into our marriages and relate to our spouses out of them. He continues to attack us, sometimes through our spouse, as he seeks to devour us, not just tempt us or cause us to stumble, but to devour us.

The Eldridges share their own wake-up call.

> We thought the plot was, "Love God. Love each other. And everything will work out!" Our naïveté nearly cost us our marriage. We learned the hard way (do any of us ever really learn any other way?) that there is a whole lot more going on here. We had to face our brokenness. That was a shock. We had to confront our style of relating. That was humbling. We needed to learn that this is a far more dangerous story than we thought, that there is much more at stake. And maybe the biggest eye-opener of all—we learned we had an enemy.[1]

Instead of fighting each other, we must fight the real enemy together. This begins on our knees. If we can pray with our husbands about the conflicts we're encountering, it will be even more powerful; however, if our relationship is not in that place or he's not at that place, we can still pray like crazy. We may not think much about praying for our conflicts when life is going well because we're really not in the midst of it, but we can continue to pray and ask God even in those peaceful times to give us a united heart and give us the continued desire to work through conflicts with respect and love.

Then when we find ourselves in the middle of a battle, big or little, we can stop and pray together, stop and pray aloud, or just pray silently in our hearts. *God, help us through this, convict us both of what is wrong and right, show me how to respond with love and respect, help us to recognize the real enemy here and not let him win. Please bring healing and forgiveness. Be with us in this and draw us to you and use this to draw us closer to each other.*

Pray for:

- wisdom;
- peace;
- forgiveness;
- the ability to forgive;
- God to show common ground—common goals in the struggle;
- God to help you understand and remember that your spouse is not the enemy;
- the ability to see and resist the real enemy;
- healing;
- conviction of wrong;
- the ability to see, hear, and understand your husband's perspective;
- a united heart;
- perseverance to fight for the marriage when you want to quit.

Journal

- In what areas do you and your husband have the most conflict? Are certain subjects especially touchy? How can you pray for these?
- How have you seen the devil attempt to divide you and your husband? How have you fought him? What can you do to recognize the enemy and fight him? -remind self what's God's will & voice
  make thoughts obey Jesus
- Are there areas of your own life that need healing in order to help with the conflict in your marriage? For example, if you battle the lie that no one cares about you, this will always be a trigger with your husband causing you to feel like he doesn't care even when that's not what he's saying.
- Ask God to reveal to you anything for which you need to forgive your husband. Make a list. Write down all the wrongs he's done and hurts he's caused. Then give the list to God and burn it.
- Ask God to reveal to you anything that you need to confess to your husband and ask his forgiveness about. Make a list. Take it to your spouse and tell him that you're sorry and ask his forgiveness.

9/2017
I am so distan
him that to mention his name builds up resistance in me. We're not connected I feel (1) resentment & resistance towards him. We disagree on many things it seems, but especially (2) money. I think we need to have our (3) own money after we pay bills.
PRAYER: (1) Lord, You said we are one flesh & I am feeling resistance & resentment. Show me what's in me to make me feel this way. (2) Make us see eye to eye on money. (3) Tell us if we should have our own $ or not and how to deal w/ the frustration of wanting to spend w/o his input/overseeing
Reveal anything I need to ask Lester for forgiveness for & what to forgive him for.

1. John and Stasi Eldredge, *Love and War: Finding the Marriage You've Dreamed Of* (Colorado Springs, Colo.: WaterBrook, 2009), 90.

Praying Like Crazy Together

They are moments I treasure. I feel close to Tim. Loved by him. We feel like a team, fighting for our children together or praying for a church family we're about to serve.

They are the moments we pray together.

Our living room became holy ground as we surrounded Josh, laid our hands on him, and prayed for him and the struggles and doubts he was facing. It felt like parenting at its best.

I was struggling. Overwhelmed by the negative thoughts that were beating me up, giving me a sense of hopelessness. I recognized it as a spiritual battle and asked my husband to pray for me. Tim held me tight and prayed for me, asking God to bind the devil and speak words of courage and truth into the threatening darkness. Peace filled my thoughts; I felt the negative spirit leaving and joy returning.

Typically, our prayers together are not so dramatic. I pray with him before he sings at a church or some other event. He takes my hand while we sit in the parking lot of a church where I'm about to preach and prays for me. Before each meal we share, regardless of where we are, we join hands and pray, not only for the food, but for our children and things happening in our lives.

There is a real power in a couple coming together and praying like crazy together—for each other, jobs and responsibilities, hopes and dreams, struggles and sins, children and families, for those they're ministering to, and for everything that touches their lives. There is little that can strengthen a marriage more than regularly praying together.

Unfortunately, it's not something most couples do regularly.

Why we don't

People would say that praying together is a good thing. Important. They'd like to do it, but . . .

Why don't we pray together?

For each family, the answer will be different. We may say we believe it's important and would like to, but never intentionally make it a priority or habit in our lives. Life is incredibly busy these days and just keeps getting crazier—the urgent pushes out the important. We plan to pray together, intend to pray together, but just become so busy that we forget or are too tired when we are together.

Because we are often at different places in our spiritual journey, spouses may feel intimidated by their mates' closeness to God and deep prayers. They don't feel like they can pray "as well," so they don't want to pray together.

Praying together requires authenticity and honesty; it requires an openness that some couples may struggle with. *What will he say if he knew I struggled with this problem?* Or, *I don't want her to know that I'm afraid of this.* We hide our complete selves sometimes; and because prayer would reveal who we really are and what we're really struggling with and feeling, we don't pray together.

Some spouses may not feel it's important nor have a desire to pray together. One partner may not believe in God or in prayer, so he doesn't feel a need to pray with his wife. And some just don't give it a thought.

A starting point

It may just be that we never have prayed together before, except a blessing before a meal, and are nervous about it. We're not sure what we should pray for or how it should work. Do we pray on and on and then the other person prays on and on? Do we pray conversationally, back and forth? We're not sure how, so we just don't start. Many of us may not have a lot of experience praying with other people.

So how do we get started? How do we get past all the obstacles and just pray together?

If we're already praying before meals together, we can begin there. Take that time and make it more than just a blessing for a meal, but each of us taking a moment to pray—for whatever is on our hearts and minds at that minute. Nothing long. Just keep it simple.

As we begin praying together, it will become more natural, and our prayer times will become longer as we find more things we want to pray about together. At that point, we may need to choose a new time to pray together when we have a little longer to pray.

We may begin praying together for each other and our children, if we have them (no matter what their ages), before we head out the door in the morning. Again, nothing long. Just praying specifically for anything that the other person is encountering that day, for their witness at work, problems they're having, the people they'll influence, and protection. It'd be a great time to ask, "How can I pray for you and your day today?"

Then at the end of the day, we may want to come together to thank God for His protection and leading. It's good not to ask only for things together, but to also praise and thank God.

There will be obstacles

Tim and I decided to pray together every evening before bed. It lasted about a week. I fell asleep one night while he was still praying. Another night we weren't ready for bed at the same time. It seemed every night something different happened that made it difficult or frustrating to pray together. And we just gave up.

Our experience isn't unique. Obstacles will get in the way of praying together. We have an enemy, and one of the last things he wants us to do is to join forces and pray together. He knows the impact that would have on us individually and as a couple, as well as the effect it would have on our families, friends, churches, and communities. He will do anything he can to prevent couples from praying together—sleepiness, an unexpected phone call, a deadline that has to be met, a sick child, a disagreement that causes you to not want to talk to each other, let alone pray together, etc. He does not want us to pray together.

We can ask God to bind the devil and not allow him to prevent our time together or hinder it in any way, asking Him to open our eyes to the devil's attacks and not let him win.

God will protect us, but we will also have to fight for it. And we'll fight for the time to pray together only when we realize how important it is and what a blessing it is. When I hear Tim pray for me, I feel loved, valued, and seen. He thanks God for me and certain characteristics of mine and prays specifically for things important to me. I pray for him the same way, thanking God for the man he is, listing some of his specific characteristics, and then praying for the projects he's working on, his music ministry, classes, and whatever else I know is on his heart.

We fight for the time by committing to it and not letting obstacles stand in our way. If we miss one day, we try again the next day, not giving up. We give praying together priority in our lives.

But he doesn't want to

I've had many wives tell me that they wished their husbands would pray with them, but they don't. Many guys just feel uncomfortable praying with their wives. Women often pray with an intimacy and familiarity with God that men may not share. They may not know how to just "talk" to God, and they worry about what their wives will think. So they avoid it.

Even if your husband is reluctant to pray aloud with you, you can still ask him, "How can I pray for you today?" Or, "What's happening in your life today that I can be praying about for you?" Later, follow up by asking about what happened. He'll recognize that you are truly praying for him and care about what happens in his day.

Then risk asking him to pray for you. At first, you may just ask him to pray on his own about something for you. I've asked Tim, "When you think about me today, can you pray about the meeting I have at two this afternoon? I'm a bit nervous about it."

Other times you may say, "I'm struggling right now. Could you pray for me right now?" Or, "I'm really concerned about our daughter; could we pray together for her right now?"

This is another thing to take to God. Ask God to give your husband the desire to pray together. Talk to your husband about it. Let him know how important it is to you. Tell him that it may feel awkward at first, but that you really want to give it a try. Trust God. Trust His timing. Allow Him to grow both of you in this area.

Praying is an intimate thing. It will be important to not criticize each other or "help" each other pray "better." Prayer is honest communication with God. There is no "right way" or perfect formula. As we pray, God will guide us and teach us to pray in ways that will enable us to grow closer to Him and trust Him more.

A cord of three

Praying together is one of the most powerful things a

couple can do together. We can pray for our children, our families, those we want to see accept salvation, our church, our pastor and his family, our friends, our coworkers, our community, and, most important, each other.

Imagine what would happen if at the beginning of a disagreement with each other, we stopped and prayed, asking God to bring unity, convict us each of right and wrong, help us to see the real enemy, and reach a solution that causes our marriage to win. Imagine going through the trials of parenting during the teen and young adult years, praying together for your children. Or imagine the joy of seeing a family you've been praying for accept Jesus and then watch them be baptized together.

My parents had a wooden plate hanging on our dining room wall for years when I was growing up. Praying hands were carved into the plate. The quote on it said, "A family that prays together, stays together." That quote paraphrases a verse in Ecclesiastes: "A cord of three strands is not quickly broken" (4:12, NIV). When husbands and wives unite in prayer together with God, amazing things will happen.

Pray for:

- God to give you both the desire to pray together;
- protection from those things that will get in the way;
- God to bind the devil away and not allow him to prevent your prayer time or hinder it in any way.

Journal

- Recount a time or two when you and your husband prayed together, if you have. What did you pray for? What drew you together in prayer? What did it mean to you?

Praying Like Crazy for Your Husband

- If you and your husband did pray together, what would you want to pray about?
- What would you like your husband to pray about for you? Make a list. Give it to him and ask him if he would pray for these things for you. Ask him if there are things you can pray about for him.

Giving Him to God

When I first talked to Karen Pearson of Pacific Press® about the idea of writing a book about praying for your husband, I thought, *This shouldn't be too hard. I've been praying for Tim since we began dating thirty years ago.* Praying for all three of my guys has always been an important part of my life. I pray every day and throughout each day for them. And have prayed for a myriad of things for each of them.

I knew I wanted this book to be different from *Praying Like Crazy for Your Kids.* There was no point writing a book about praying for your husbands if it was just like praying for your kids. There had to be unique aspects about praying for your spouse—ways of praying that were different from praying for your kids, despite that we will pray for many of the same things.

I never anticipated what a journey this project would be for me. Or the ways God would convict me and speak to me through it.

As I began praying, thinking, and writing, I was struck with the knowledge that as wives, we are able to pray for our husbands in ways that no one else can because we know them better than anyone else does. We know them. We know their moods, their habits, their good qualities as well as their flaws. We have an inside seat to see what they struggle with, how they handle things, the temptations they wrestle with—and give in to. I believe we have a responsibility to pray for them. If we don't pray like crazy for them, who will?

Surrendering

But I also realized that too often when I pray for Tim, I pray that God will change him into the man I think he should be. I wouldn't necessarily admit that to myself; I'm sure I would say that I want what God wants. But as I look at the ways I've prayed, I know it's true. I've been known to complain to God about Tim. Ask, *Why does he have to be this way? Why can't he be like that instead?*

I believe that when we see our husbands struggling with something or know a specific need, we do need to take it to God and ask God to work in their lives. But we also need to trust God, asking for His will, His timing, His conviction, and His leading—not asking God to make the outcome look like what we want it to look like. Prayer isn't about my getting to custom-design my husband. Prayer is trusting that God will do what He knows is best for my husband—and for me.

Prayer requires me to surrender Tim to God. Trusting God to work in his life and grow him into the man He designed him to be. And also trusting God that Tim is the man whom God chose for my life. Such a belief means that even when Tim doesn't match up to what I think I want him to be, I believe that he is who God planned for me now—to help me grow and stretch and become the woman God created me to be.

As I pray and surrender Tim to God, I lay down all my dreams for him, too, and trust God's dreams for him. Tim has an awesome gift for music. I would love to see him pursue that professionally—I know he would bless others with his gift. I'd like to see him find a few other guys, who are as passionate about music as he is, to form a quartet and see where it leads. Because I dream big, I picture them traveling in a bus and giving concerts all over the country. I can even imagine them singing during a Gaither Homecoming. We've talked about it. I've given him ideas of how to make that happen. (Unsolicited but graciously listened to.) Ultimately, it's between him and God. I have to trust that if this is a dream God has for Tim, He will give him ideas and lead him to the right people and places to make that dream happen. But God's dream may be for Tim to use his gift in the small churches scattered across Pennsylvania where he sometimes sings—and not include touring the country on a bus. I must surrender my dream for Tim and ask God to make His dreams come true. I have to remind myself that God knows Tim even better than I do and will do everything out of His deep love for him.

Surrendering Tim and allowing God to do what He wants, when He wants, according to His plan for Tim, also requires me to surrender my marriage and what I think it should look like. Tim and I are two very different people. We "speak" love to each other in different ways. I write love notes and leave them here and there. He changes the oil in my car and makes sure it's ready for my next trip. I want to go out on dates and have fun. He likes snuggling on the couch and watching a movie.

As most wives have experienced, there have been times that Tim's and my differences have been frustrating. Times when I wanted him to be more talkative or more romantic—send me flowers or ask me all kinds of questions about a project so I know he is interested. I know that many times I have frustrated him as well. I've been known to talk on and on and get excited about some idea—and he'd like me to calm down and not start on another new project.

I don't know if Tim has complained to God about me, but I've complained to God about him. I've asked God to make him different and to make the marriage more the way I want it to be. I'm sure sometimes it sounded like whining. It definitely didn't sound like surrender and asking God for His will to be done.

So I've been asking God to forgive me. And have been learning to surrender Tim, our marriage, my dreams for him and for us, and trusting that God is working in both of our lives and working in our marriage. Total surrender requires me to trust God completely and learn to live contentedly and with peace and even joy in this moment, regardless of whether it looks like my plan or not.

It's pretty amazing. God brings two flawed, wounded people together and uses those flaws and wounds to grow each other. He longs for the best for both of us. He can be trusted. He loves us each more than anyone else has ever loved us. Even each other. He loves Tim more than I do and wants more for him than I possibly could. And He can make it all happen. I just have to surrender and trust.

Being able to surrender completely to God means that I have to know God. Really know Him. I have to believe that He loves me unconditionally and completely. I need to trust that love enough to believe He would never do anything to hurt us, would never allow anything that He won't redeem, and that He will never forsake us or leave us. I can surrender Tim to God when I know beyond a shadow of a doubt that God will do what's best for Tim. I can trust God with our marriage—even when it's difficult or not quite the way I want it to be, knowing that He will redeem the hard parts, use all of it to refine and grow us, and will continue working in us to make our marriage what He desires.

Surrender is really a relief. It puts God in control, not me. I don't have to fix Tim or be responsible for his happiness. I just need to love him well and pray like crazy for him.

Surrendering doesn't mean giving up

Surrender doesn't mean that I'm giving up on praying for the things that I want for my husband or that I stop fighting in prayer for the temptations, struggles, and relationship challenges in my husband's life and just say, "Oh, that's just how it is." I continue to pray for those things. There are some things that I want for Tim's life that I never stop praying for.

Surrender doesn't mean that a husband engages in sin, like pornography, anger, or a substance addiction, and a wife stops praying when nothing changes, saying, "This must be God's will because He's not answering my prayers." God's Word is clear on many topics, such as sin, character, relationships, and the type of people we're supposed to be. We don't give up or give in when nothing happens; we keep praying. We may want to consider fasting and prayer for those things that have a real hold on their hearts, but we continue fighting for our husbands in prayer.

Surrender does mean that I trust God and ask for His will. I honestly pray what's on my heart for Tim, telling God what I want and what I think, but ultimately asking for His will and then trusting that God will do what's eternally best for Tim. I continually remind myself that even when I can't see anything happening, God is answering prayer, He is at work, and I need to trust Him.

For instance, I can pray for Tim and his music and ask God to open the doors He wants, using him to bless others and to draw people closer to God. I can talk to God about my dream of a music ministry for Tim, but in the end, I must trust God to open the doors *He* has for Tim and let it go, believing God has a plan for Tim and knows what's best for him. I know God gave Tim a gift and can trust He will use it for His glory.

Shannon has been praying for George and his relationship with his children for years. "George was a tough dad," she shares. "He didn't spend a lot of time just playing with the kids or talking to them. He saw his role as teaching them what to do, how to do it, and growing them into good people. He lectured more than he asked questions. He was very strict with them. They often felt like their dad didn't love them or accept them because he was always pushing them to do better. Now that they're all grown and have families of their own, he really doesn't have a relationship with them. He doesn't know what to do if he's not telling them what to do," Shannon sighs. She's been praying for her husband and asking God to show him how to build a relationship with his children for years. And still she prays, waiting for things to change. "There are times when I've been mad at God for not answering, for not showing George how to be interested in the kids and not helping the kids to see that their father loves them incredibly. God and I have had a few 'talks' about this. Ultimately though, I know I can trust God. He wants a good relationship between all of them more than I do. And He alone can make it happen. So I keep praying and believing that God is at work, will draw them all close, and will redeem the hurts and wounds between them."

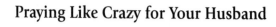

Thanking

As God and I have talked about surrender and trusting Him, He's also reminded me that I need to be thankful. It's so easy to focus on the negatives—the things I want changed. Again, I need to give those to God, surrender them to Him, trusting that He will work out His will in those areas, but I also need to focus on the positives. I need to spend more time thanking God for Tim and the things happening in his life.

Praying prayers of thankfulness isn't some requirement from a God who wants to be noticed and appreciated. God doesn't have an ego that needs feeding. Rather, He knows what thankfulness does in our hearts—how it changes us.

When all I'm doing is praying about the things that drive me crazy, I can get negative and discontent in my marriage. I can easily forget the positives and the things I love about Tim. Thankfulness helps keep it all in perspective. Thankfulness changes *me.* I believe God asks us to be thankful because He knows how it benefits us.

We don't always think about being thankful. We may easily take our prayer requests to God, but we have to intentionally think about being thankful. It's easy to make our list of what we want God to do and forget to thank Him for what He's done. As we purposely take time to thank God, to look for the ways He's working, to remind ourselves of our husband's good qualities, and to be thankful for these things, it will encourage us and help us see that God is answering prayers and has blessed us.

So I thank God for getting Tim through his first semester of college—for giving him the perseverance and courage to go back and stick with it. I thank God for how He's used Tim at school. Tim has encouraged kids in his class, sought out the ones who seem to not have friends and talked to them. I thank God for Tim's commitment to our family; he is an incredibly hardworking, dependable, loyal man. These are all qualities I can thank God for.

As I grow a thankful heart in prayer, it spills over. I thank Tim. I tell him I admire his perseverance with school—there were days when it was tough, and I know he must've wondered if he could do it. I tell him I appreciate having a husband who can fix the little things around the house that break down. Not only does it do my heart good and remind me who this man is and how I love him, but it encourages Tim, helping him feel appreciated and respected.

Thankfulness needs to be an important part of our prayer life. It will make a difference in us, helping us to experience peace and joy as we watch our Father work.

Praying like crazy

There is no magic formula to prayer. No right words to say for you to get exactly what you asked for. No "if I do this, God will do this," one, two, three. Prayer is a relationship. It requires faith to trust that God will answer. It requires faith to believe that God loves your husband—and you—more than you can comprehend and will move heaven and earth for you. He's already given His Son for us. He didn't allow His Son to die for us and then walk away and leave us on our own. He wouldn't pay such a great price for us, while we were sinners, only to give up on us now. He loves us. He cares about us. He is working in our lives. He is preparing us to live with Him for eternity and daily growing and refining who we are.

Praying like crazy for our husbands changes things. It changes us as we learn to surrender and trust God, watching for the ways that He is working and thanking Him for it. It changes our husbands as we give God permission to work in their lives. It changes our marriages, helping us love our husbands well, making us a team, working together, supporting each other as we head toward the finish line.

God will not say Yes to everything we ask for in prayer. The answer may seem long in coming, but God will always reveal more of Himself in answer to our prayers. His ultimate goal is for us to know Him, really know Him, as intimately as human beings can know God. As we pray like crazy, we will learn just how crazy God is about us.

Pray for:

- God to give you what it takes to completely surrender your husband to Him;
- God to make His dreams for your spouse come true, surrendering your own;
- Him to make your marriage what He designed marriage to be;
- Him to use your marriage, including your differences and even the frustrating parts, to refine you and make you the woman He created you to be;
- those things you appreciate about your husband, thanking God for him, his character, the things he does, the ways he loves you.

Journal

- Are there things that you need to surrender to God concerning your husband?

Giving Him to God

- How easy is it for you to trust that God will do what's best in response to your prayers? If it's hard, what makes it hard to trust Him? What would it take for you to completely surrender to God and believe He will do what's best for you and for your husband?
- Make a list of the things that you are thankful for about your husband. Include character traits, things he does, quirks, etc. Thank God daily for your husband and look for opportunities to thank your husband.

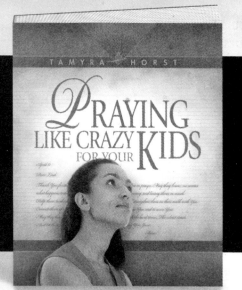